Improving the Environment

An Evaluation of DOE's Environmental Management Program

Committee to Evaluate the Science, Engineering, and
Health Basis of the Department of Energy's
Environmental Management Program

National Research Council

National Academy Press
Washington, D.C. 1995

NATIONAL ACADEMY PRESS • 2101 Constitution Ave., N.W. • Washington, D.C. 20418

NOTICE: This volume was produced as part of a project approved by the Governing Board of the National Research Council, whose members are drawn from the councils of the National Academy of Sciences, the National Academy of Engineering, and the Institute of Medicine. The members of the expert committees were chosen for their special competencies and with regard for appropriate balance. This report has been reviewed by a group other than the authors according to procedures approved by the NRC and the Report Review Committee.

The **National Academy of Sciences** (NAS) is a private, nonprofit, self-perpetuating society of distinguished scholars engaged in scientific and engineering research, dedicated to the furtherance of science and technology and to their use for the general welfare. Under the authority of the charter granted to it by Congress in 1863, the Academy has a working mandate that calls on it to advise the federal government on scientific and technical matters. Dr. Bruce M. Alberts is president of the NAS.

The **National Academy of Engineering** (NAE) was established in 1964, under the charter of the NAS, as a parallel organization of distinguished engineers. It is autonomous in its administration and in the selection of members, sharing with the NAS its responsibilities for advising the federal government. The National Academy of Engineering also sponsors engineering programs aimed at meeting national needs, encourages education and research, and recognizes the superior achievements of engineers. Dr. Harold Leibowitz is president of the NAE.

The **Institute of Medicine** (IOM) was established in 1970 by the NAS to secure the services of eminent members of appropriate professions in the examination of policy matters pertaining to the health of the public. The Institute acts under the responsibility given to the NAS in its congressional charter to be an adviser to the federal government and, on its own initiative, to identify issues of medical care, research, and education. Dr. Kenneth I. Shine is president of the IOM.

The **National Research Council** (NRC) was organized by the NAS in 1916 to associate the broad community of science and technology with the Academy's purposes of furthering knowledge and advising the federal government. Functioning in accordance with general policies determined by the Academy, the Council has become the principle operating agency of both the NAS and the NAE in providing services to the government, the public, and the scientific and engineering communities. The Council is administered jointly by both Academies and the IOM. Dr. Bruce M. Alberts and Dr. Harold Leibowitz are chairman and vice chairman, respectively, of the NRC.

This project was supported by the U.S. Department of Energy.

Library of Congress Catalog Card Number 95-73219
International Standard Book Number 0-309-05440

Internet Access: This report is available on the National Academy of Sciences' Internet host. It may be accessed via World Wide Web at http://www.nas.edu, via Gopher at gopher.nas.edu, or via FTP at ftp.nas.edu.

Available from: National Academy Press, 2101 Constitution Avenue, N.W., Box 285, Washington, D.C. 20055
1-800-624-6242 or 202-334-3313 (in Washington metropolitan area)

Printed in the United States of America

Committee to Evaluate the Science, Engineering, and Health Basis of the Department of Energy's Environmental Management Program

Synthesis Subcommittee

JOHN F. AHEARNE, Lecturer in Public Policy, Duke University
ANDREW P. CAPUTO, Attorney, Natural Resources Defense Council
EDWIN H. CLARK II, President, Clean Sites, Inc.
DON CLAY, President, Don Clay Associates, Inc.
DOUGLAS M. COSTLE, Chairman and Distinguished Fellow, Institute for Sustainable Communities
JAMES R. CURTISS, Attorney, Winston & Strawn
FRANK L. PARKER, Distinguished Professor of Environmental and Water Resources Engineering, Vanderbilt University
VICTORIA J. TSCHINKEL, Senior Consultant on Environmental Issues, Landers & Parsons
JOHN T. WHETTEN, Senior Applications Consultant, Motorola

Staff

Paul Gilman, Project Director
Deborah Stine, Project Coordinator
Patrick Sevcik, Project Assistant

Subcommittee on the Evaluation of Regulatory Measures

DON CLAY (*Chair*), President, Don Clay Associates, Inc.
ANDREW P. CAPUTO, Attorney, Natural Resources Defense Council
JAMES R. CURTISS, Attorney, Winston & Strawn
MARSHALL E. DRUMMOND, President, Eastern Washington University
DANIEL S. MILLER, First Assistant Attorney General, Colorado Department of Law
BERNARD J. REILLY, Corporate Council, DuPont Legal
MARY RIVELAND, Director, Washington State Department of Ecology

Staff

Ray Wassel, Senior Program Officer
Ruth Danoff, Project Assistant

iii

Subcommittee on Priority-Setting, Timing, and Staging

EDWIN H. CLARK II (*Chair*), President, Clean Sites, Inc.
HUGH J. CAMPBELL, JR., Environmental Manager, DuPont
MARY R. ENGLISH, Associate Director, Energy, Environment, and Resources Center, University of Tennessee
DONALD R. GIBSON, Department Manager, Systems Analysis, TRW Environmental Safety Systems
ROBERT E. HAZEN, Chief, Bureau of Risk Assessment, New Jersey Department of Environmental Protection
THOMAS LESCHINE, Associate Professor, School of Marine Affairs, University of Washington
ROBERT H. NEILL, Director, Environmental Evaluation Group, New Mexico
LYNNE M. PRESLO, Senior Vice President, Technical Programs, Earth Tech
ANNE E. SMITH, Principal and Vice President, Decision Focus, Inc.
MERVYN L. TANO, General Counsel, Council of Energy Resource Tribes

Staff
Robert Andrews, Senior Program Officer
Patricia Jones, Project Assistant

Subcommittee on Utilization of Science, Engineering, and Technology

FRANK L. PARKER (*Chair*), Distinguished Professor of Environmental and Water Resources Engineering, Vanderbilt University
JOHN F. AHEARNE, Lecturer in Public Policy, Duke University
CHARLES B. ANDREWS, Vice President, S.S. Papadopulos & Associates, Inc.
EDGAR BERKEY, President, National Environmental Technology Applications Center, University of Pittsburgh Applied Research Center
HAROLD K. FORSEN, Senior Vice President (retired), Bechtel Hanford, Inc.
WALTER W. KOVALICK, Director, Technology Innovation Office, Office of Solid Waste and Emergency Response, U.S. Environmental Protection Agency
MICHAEL L. MASTRACCI, Director, Innovative Technology Programs, TECHMATICS, Inc.
PHILIP A. PALMER, Senior Environmental Fellow, DuPont Specialty Chemicals, E.I. du Pont de Nemours & Company
REBECCA T. PARKIN, Director of Scientific, Professional, and Section Affairs, American Public Health Administration
ALFRED SCHNEIDER, Professor of Nuclear Engineering (retired), Georgia Institute of Technology

Preface

In a letter that I received on January 11, 1995, Thomas Grumbly, U.S. Department of Energy (DOE) Assistant Secretary for Environmental Management, requested the assistance of the Academy in addressing remedial-action and waste-management problems that his office and the nation are now facing as a result of 50 years of nuclear weapons development and testing (see Appendix A). These are problems that require a re-engineering of systems and a re examination of the scientific, engineering, and institutional barriers to achieving cost-effective and safe stewardship of the nation's resources.

In response to this request, the National Research Council established the Committee to Evaluate the Science, Engineering, and Health Basis of the Department of Energy's Environmental Management Program. Four subcommittees were formed to address topics outlined in Mr. Grumbly's request. The subcommittees were assigned the following topics:

- Evaluation of regulatory measures.
- Setting priorities, timing, and staging.
- Utilization of science, engineering, and technology.
- Integration of science, engineering, and health in program implementation.

Subcommittee membership (see Appendix C) included a unique combination of those from the scientific and technological community and participants knowledgeable about the concerns of the various stakeholder groups that are involved in DOE's environmental remediation process. The knowledge of these stakeholders included substantive expertise and site-specific experience with the process involved in DOE's environmental remediation program. These individuals, having experience in state and federal agencies involved in monitoring DOE's cleanup operations, national and local citizen, environmental, and American Indian groups, and DOE's citizen taskforces, were able to provide a unique contribution as members of each subcommittee. Members of the subcommittees also included individuals who have addressed similar problems in industry and individuals with background in federal and state government management, including members of the National Academy of Public Administration.

In terms of process, each subcommittee held a workshop which offered an opportunity for public input, followed immediately by a meeting of the subcommittee to develop a brief report. Prior background readings, knowledge, and discussions resulting from the workshops provided the basis for the subcommittees' deliberations. The four subcommittee reports were submitted to a synthesis committee which included the chairs of each of the subcommittees and selected members to provide a spectrum of viewpoints. The subcommittees' complete reports, as well as that of the synthesis committee, follow. Though the memberships of the subcommittees were selected to provide different viewpoints and experience and each of the subcommittees deliberated separately, there was surprising consensus among the reports of the four subcommittees. Beyond the synthesis committee report, no attempt was made to conform the results of the four separate subcommittee deliberations. The reader should look to the individual reports for further detail and for additional recommendations and observations.

Although these reports represent the work of each of the committees, they benefited greatly from the support of the National Research Council staff, specifically, Paul Gilman, who helped refine all the reports, and Deborah Stine, who coordinated the various project activities for the overall report. Each subcommittee was also helped by its staff, Ray Wassel for Regulatory Measures, Tamae Wong for Integration, Stephen Parker and Karyanil Thomas for Utilization, and Robert Andrews for Priority-Setting. In addition, Patrick Sevcik, Helen Chin, Ruth Danoff, and Patricia Jones provided invaluable support.

The National Research Council also acknowledges with appreciation presentations made at the workshops by the persons listed in Appendix D.

BRUCE ALBERTS
President, National Academy of Sciences
Chairman, National Research Council

Contents

Part I
Synthesis Report

SYNTHESIS SUBCOMMITTEE

JOHN F. AHEARNE, Lecturer in Public Policy, Duke University
ANDREW P. CAPUTO, Attorney, Natural Resources Defense Council
EDWIN H. CLARK, President, Clean Sites, Inc.
DON CLAY, President, Don Clay Associates, Inc.
DOUGLAS M. COSTLE, Chairman and Distinguished Fellow, Institute for Sustainable Communities
JAMES R. CURTISS, Attorney, Winston & Strawn
FRANK L. PARKER, Distinguished Professor of Environmental and Water Resources Engineering, Vanderbilt University
VICTORIA J. TSCHINKEL, Senior Consultant on Environmental Issues, Landers & Parsons
JOHN T. WHETTEN, Senior Applications Consultant, Motorola

Staff

Paul Gilman, Project Director
Deborah Stine, Project Coordinator
Patrick Sevcik, Project Assistant

Introduction

In a letter to the President of the National Academy of Sciences, Thomas Grumbly, U.S. Department of Energy Assistant Secretary of Environmental Management, requested the assistance of the Academy in addressing remedial action and waste management problems that his office and the nation are now facing as a result of 50 years of nuclear weapons development and testing (see Appendix A). These problems require a re-engineering of systems and a re-examination of the scientific, engineering, and institutional barriers to achieving cost-effective and safe stewardship of the Department's resources. In response to the request, the National Research Council of the Academy established the Committee to Evaluate the Science, Engineering, and Health Basis of the Department of Energy's Environmental Management Program. Four subcommittees were formed to address topics outlined in Mr. Grumbly's request. The subcommittees were assigned the following topics:

- Evaluation of regulatory measures.
- Setting priorities, timing, and staging.
- Utilization of science, engineering, and technology.
- Integration of science, engineering, and health in the implementation of the Environmental Management Program.

Each subcommittee held a workshop that was followed immediately by a meeting to develop a brief report. Information and discussions resulting from the workshops as well as background documents reviewed in preparation for the workshops informed the subcommittees' deliberations. The subcommittees' four reports were submitted to the synthesis subcommittee that was

3

formed to draw key points from each of them. This is the report of the synthesis subcommittee; the subcommittees' complete reports follow. Though the memberships of the subcommittees were selected to provide different viewpoints and experience there was surprising consensus among the subcommittees, though no attempt was made to conform the results of their separate deliberations. The reader should look to the different reports for further detail on the issues raised here and for additional recommendations and observations.

PROBLEMS ASSOCIATED WITH THE DEPARTMENT'S LEGACY

The United States involvement in nuclear weapons development for the last 50 years has resulted in the development of a vast research, production, and testing network known as the nuclear weapons complex; over $300 billion (in 1995 dollars) has been invested in the activities of this complex. The Department has begun the environmental remediation of the complex, which will encompass radiological and nonradiological hazards, vast volumes of contaminated water and soil, and over 7,000 contaminated structures (DOE, 1995a). The Department must characterize, treat, and dispose of hazardous and radioactive wastes that have been accumulating for more than 50 years at 120 sites in 36 states and territories. By 1995, the Department had spent about $23 billion in identifying and characterizing its waste, managing it, and assessing the remediation necessary for its sites and facilities. The Department estimates that the remedial action at Department sites (not including groundwater cleanup, currently operating facilities and Naval facilities) could cost a total of $200–350 billion and take at least 75 years to complete (DOE, 1995b). According to the estimates of the total cost, 49% would go to waste management, 28% to environmental restoration, 10% to nuclear material and facility stabilization, and 5% to technology development with the remaining 8% for activities such as site security, transportation, and other landlord activities.

Environmental Management is also responsible for conducting the program for waste minimization and pollution prevention for the Department. The variety and volume of the Department's current activities make this effort a challenge itself. The Department has nearly 30 contractor operated laboratories employing about 50,000 people who are engaged in the full spectrum of scientific and engineering disciplines. Moreover, the Department is engaged in the largest weapons-dismantlement effort in its history. Current programmatic activities in nuclear weapons, energy, and basic research, as well as current remediation efforts are the subject of an initiative announced by Secretary O'Leary to reduce by 50% the amount of toxic waste that the Department's facilities produce by the year 1999 (DOE, 1995c).

The Department's Office of Environmental Management was established in 1989 to deal with the environmental legacy of the Department's nuclear weapons program. The Environmental Management Program has six goals which have been established by Assistant Secretary Grumbly:

• To eliminate and manage urgent risks in the system.
• To emphasize the health and safety of workers and the public.
• To establish a system that includes sound managerial and financial controls.
• To demonstrate tangible results.
• To focus technology development on identifying and overcoming obstacles to progress.
• To establish a stronger partnership between the Department and its stakeholders.

The Department's historical culture of secrecy and its contamination problems at nuclear weapons sites have combined to affect public attitudes and public opinion in a profound way. Citizens have expressed concern at the community and national levels about the potential health and environmental impacts of conditions in the nuclear weapons complex, urging that sites be cleaned up. Technology to characterize and remediate contaminated soil or water or to treat, store, and dispose of accumulated waste safely does not always exist. For most sites, waste-disposal standards and goals for cleanup levels for the environment have not been developed, agreed to, or applied (OTA, 1991).

FUNDAMENTAL PRECEPTS FOR THE DEPARTMENT'S ENVIRONMENTAL MANAGEMENT PROGRAM

Several fundamental precepts about the Department's Environmental Management Program should be understood before one attempts to analyze the program in an informed manner.

Risk Associated with the Program

The contamination at the weapons complex is serious and extensive. The biggest risks are those to workers, and these risks arise from addressing contamination and waste problems and from managing the contamination or waste in place (OTA, 1991; Blush and Heitman, 1995; CERE, 1995). Examples of these significant worker risks include plutonium that is packaged in unstable forms, rooms that are heavily contaminated with plutonium and other radionuclides, and spent fuel that is corroding in cooling ponds.

Public health is at less immediate risk than is worker safety, largely because most waste and contamination is being managed and contained at present. There is still cause for real concern in this area, though, particularly over the medium to long-term. The current mechanisms for managing and containing potential public health risks (such as controlling access to the site) will degrade long before the contamination becomes benign. Some contaminants have moved offsite (such as plutonium-contaminated soil at Rocky Flats) or are in the process of moving offsite (such as contaminated groundwater at Hanford moving toward the Columbia River). Because of a lack of agreed-upon cleanup standards, commitments made before problems were understood, and limited risk studies, in many cases it is not possible to separate truly hazardous conditions from those where contamination is measurable, but not a serious health risk. Nevertheless, this uncertainty must not be used as a rationale for not moving ahead aggressively with cleanup programs.

Cost of the Program

The magnitude of the cleanup job facing the Department is usually communicated by simply repeating the annual budget for the activity, $6.5 billion. The shocking fact about that amount is that fully $4 billion of it is spent simply to maintain facilities and sites in an attempt to contain contamination and to maintain old facilities for which funds for decommissioning are unavailable. The Department is running in place and spending $4 billion a year to do it, and this figure will grow if nothing is done to increase site remediation and facility decontamination and decommissioning.

Length of the Program

The expectation that the remediation process will continue for at least 75 years (DOE, 1995b) affects the approach to planning, managing, and technology selection and development. Stabilization of a site now and development of a better technology, instead of detailed characterization of the site, might be the better approach to an already-costly problem. Planning and technology development must be iterative because conditions will change and new developments that will need to be factored into the Department's decision-making will take place. Priorities will change as political leadership changes. All this will make the management of the Program a continuing challenge.

The long duration of remediation should not be interpreted as a mandate for inaction, but for management and technical approaches that will change over time.

Science and Technology in the Program

Many waste-management problems in the Department lend themselves to solutions that have already found application in the private sector. Many do not. In some circumstances, technologies and processes for safe and efficient remediation or waste minimization do not exist. In other cases, the development of new technology and processes might substantially reduce the costs of, or risks associated with, remediation and waste management. An effective technology-development program focused on such opportunities is an essential element of an overall strategy for reducing the cost and speeding the pace of the Environmental Management Program.

In some cases, fundamental science questions will have to be addressed before a technology or process can be engineered. For example, improved understanding of the principles of pollutant transport in groundwater is required for important advancement in the development of groundwater-remediation technology. There is a need to involve more basic science researchers in the challenges of the Department's remediation effort. The formula is simple: Department research managers must fund long-term research programs with the most creative and innovative researchers, and the researchers must be kept involved with the "customers"—those who have the particular remediation or waste-minimization problems.

Environmental Mission or Environmental Ethic?

The Department spends more resources on its Environmental Management Program than on any other activity, and environmental management is often described as one of the Department's central missions. However, the Department should view its remedial activities as industry does, not as a central mission, but rather as a job that must be completed so that the Department can return to its more basic missions. Viewing it this way will help keep the focus of remediation activities on efficiency and cost effectiveness rather than on creating a self-perpetuating activity.

Waste minimization and pollution prevention should be embraced as integral to the performance of such missions as supporting long-term national security and science and technology development. US Industry is refocusing and substantially broadening its vision of how to do its business in this manner, and the Department should do likewise (see also pp. 107–108, 154). For current products and processes, that means setting pollution-prevention goals and acknowledging that the most effective way to reach them is to make environmental criteria a part of experiment, process, and product designs.

ENVIRONMENTAL MANAGEMENT'S NOTABLE INITIATIVES

A number of initiatives are rapidly introducing change into a system that was established during the Cold War. It is too early to assess their effectiveness and how long they will last, but their principles and general direction are encouraging. In our recommendations, we note some of the improvements, and we recognize that change will continue even during the final preparation of this report.

Research and Development Initiative

The Office of Energy Research and the Office of Environmental Management have made a commitment to create a new program designed to integrate a long-term research effort into the Environmental Management Program to make crucial advances. The Congress has allocated $50 million of the Environmental Management Program funding for this effort. Such collaboration is the kind of integration recommended in all the subcommittees' reports. Keys to the success of the effort include consistency of funding, a commitment from program managers in the Department to make it a truly new effort rather than a repackaging of existing programs, and a broad outreach to universities and industries and foreign researchers in partnership with the Department's National Laboratories (see also pp. 117–119, 121–122, 150–151). An example of this kind of an effort is the creation of the Consortium on Risk Evaluation with Stakeholder Participation (CRESP), which resulted from recommendations of an earlier National Research Council report (NRC, 1994).

Contractor Relations

Establishing a system that is managerially and financially in control is one of Environmental Management's stated goals. One example of how it is attempting to achieve that goal is the introduction of a contract-reform initiative. Several basic elements of the reform are increased competition; renewed focus on the protection of workers, the public, and the environment; a results-oriented focus; and performance-based incentives. In recent months, a performance-based integrated contract adopting the elements of the contract-reform initiative has been introduced and implemented at the Rocky Flats Environmental Technology Site. Some workshop participants emphasized that it is too early to predict the effectiveness of the new contract, but all subcommittees strongly supported the intentions and direction of the contract-reform effort (see also pp. 34–35, 79, 147–149). Key to the success of this effort will be a clear written statement by Department leadership of the desired relationship between Department employees and contractors.

Budgeting Process

One notable initiative has been the integration of risk and long-term cost data into budgeting. While we did not undertake a critical review of the technical elements of the report, the publication of *Risks and the Risk Debate:*

Searching for Common Ground, "The First Step" (DOE, 1995d) the broad intent of this effort is indeed an important first step for integrating risk assessment into budgeting. Current efforts to integrate options to reduce the cost of maintaining sites and facilities in a safe status while awaiting remediation, which will necessarily incorporate cost-benefit analysis, will further strengthen the analytical basis of Environmental Management's budgeting process. Environmental Management has correctly recognized that without stakeholder acceptance and consensus on both the process and the outcomes, improved analytical techniques and better factual information will be of less value (although such techniques and information can serve to inform the stakeholders in those decisions).

Public Participation

The Department has made a substantial effort to improve the participation of its many stakeholders in its deliberations and decision-making, and the Secretary has shown exemplary leadership in this regard (see also pp. 69–70, 155). The result is a perceptible improvement in the credibility of the Department and of Environmental Management (surveys of stakeholders taken in 1992 and 1994 and presented to the Secretary of Energy's Advisory Board on October 26, 1995, showed a statistically significant change in the level of trust in the Department's Office of Environmental Management, $p = 0.0003$).

Principal Recommendations

RESULTS NEEDED NOW

There are a number of common themes and observations throughout the four subcommittee reports. One is the observation that the Department has undertaken a long-term task. Nonetheless, there is a consensus among regulators, the Department, Congress, and the public that it is time to get on with the task of cleaning up the nuclear weapons complex. While there may be a consensus to get on with the task there is no real consensus as to what that means. For some it is meeting milestones in compliance agreements and for others it means remediating contaminated soil, groundwater, and buildings, even when the process chosen may take decades and many billions of dollars to complete regardless of what compliance agreement milestones may require. This committee believes getting on with the task, whichever definition one uses, will be accomplished most effectively by implementing a process for decision-making and accountability that includes

• Having a more specific set of goals for the program (see also pp. 66–67, 108–112, 141–142).

• A process for prioritizing tasks which includes among its tools risk assessment, (which should consider the perspectives and values of stakeholders as recommended in *Building Consensus* (NRC, 1994)) and cost-benefit analysis (see also pp. 44–45, 46, 82–83, 103–104, 110, 120–121, 144–145).

• A peer-reviewed remediation and waste-minimization technology selection and development process that is responsive to the needs of those implementing the remediation (see also pp. 65, 104, 113, 116, 119, 121, 122).

• An overall organizational and management structure which both provides an opportunity for stakeholder input in each of the above activities (see also pp. 69–70, 83, 113, 146–147, 155–157) and provides incentives for stakeholders and federal and contract workers to implement these activities of the Environmental Management Program successfully (see also pp. 113, 147–149).

Responsible Stewardship

The lack of appropriate technology or a permanent solution for remediating a polluted site or facility should not be an excuse not to take appropriate steps on a near-term or interim basis. Responsible stewardship means undertaking appropriate near-term or mid-term action to remediate a site to protect the public and the environment when a permanent solution is not at hand. Communities and states that are willing to make institutional commitments to implement such plans for near-term and mid-term remedies are participating in responsible stewardship. In the absence of permanent solutions, responsible stewardship allows progress to be made by providing adequate protection against environmental and human health risks that are serious and long-lived (see also pp. 10 11, 48). It deals with waste in relatively short increments of time, say, 20 years. After such a period, existing approaches should be re-examined, and society can decide what to do for the next 20 years. Until permanent solutions are developed, actions taken as part of responsible stewardship that are irreversible should be avoided.

An example at Hanford related to decisions about contamination along the Columbia River illustrates the idea of responsible stewardship. Stakeholders have placed a high priority on unrestricted access to lands along the river. They have also acknowledged that no solution for complete remediation of the underlying groundwater exists. Therefore, work has focused on the remediation of soils and on remediating and containing sources of groundwater contamination while the long-term goal of unrestricted use of the groundwater is retained.

Another example is the approach taken to management of transuranic waste at the Idaho National Engineering Laboratory. Recently, the Department has undertaken a major effort at consolidating, repackaging, monitoring, and sheltering its transuranic waste. Instead of being exposed to the effects of weather and the possibility of corrosion and leaks, drums containing transuranic waste are stored on concrete or asphalt pads in weather-resistant structures. Much of the waste had been stored in earth-covered drums, which were expected to be needed for only a few years, until a permanent disposal site became available. The Department is now repacking drums that began to corrode or leak and is building new interim storage facilities (DOE, 1995a).

It is important to underscore that responsible stewardship should not be relied on to provide permanent solutions. Some components in radioactive waste can continue to be a threat to human health and safety for thousands of years. The National Research Council (NRC, 1995) concludes for high-level nuclear waste disposal that although it might be reasonable to assume that interim actions can be relied on for some initial period, there is no scientific basis for assuming the long-term effectiveness of institutional controls to protect against releases of the stored radioactive materials.

Land-Use Planning

Many contaminated sites and facilities could be restored to a pristine condition suitable for any desired use; or they could be restored to a point where some uses (e.g., industrial development or recreation) would pose no health risks. In other cases, when permanent remedies are unavailable, surrounding communities could be protected for the near future by interim remedial actions and fencing off sites and facilities. Each of those options is associated with different costs and benefits. Land-use decisions are relevant to the determination of regulatory measures in that different cleanup-level goals might be set for different land-use options with little or no difference in the risks posed to human health (see also pp. 42–43, 111, 112).

The Department believes that most current efforts at land-use planning are inadequate, as are the mechanisms for their implementation. In cases bound by legal obligations or commitments by the Department, some obligations and commitments may not be technically feasible. In cases not bound by legal obligations or commitments by the Department, future land use is unclear. The Department has begun working with stakeholders and regulators regarding the ultimate disposition of lands currently managed by the Department (DOE, 1995b).

We believe that effects on land use and groundwater should be among the first considerations in the planning of remediation. There is also a need for a formal decision-making framework for future land-use and cleanup standards that will provide an opportunity for consensus-based selection of appropriate data, analysis, and criteria for decision-making. The framework must include an opportunity for stakeholder input at all stages and lead to enforceable agreements that can be modified as further knowledge is gained.

If land use restrictions are to be incorporated in cleanup remedies for Department sites there must be clear assurance that the land use will in fact be controlled for the duration of the contamination. This is a serious problem for sites contaminated with long-lived radionuclides. The record of decision selecting the remedy should incorporate specific commitments by the Department designed to maintain the necessary institutional controls over the lifetime of the contamination. Where contaminants are so long-lived that such commitments are impossible, the remedy should include specific procedures designed to reassess at regular intervals the adequacy of the institutional controls and, where such reassessment detects problems, to either address the inadequacies or reopen the remedy.

The Department is extending the Comprehensive Environmental Response, Compensation and Liability Act (CERCLA)-based Environmental Protection Agency land-use directive (issued on May 25, 1995) to Resource Conservation and Recovery Act (RCRA) corrective action so that reasonably anticipated future land use is identified early in the decision-making process on the basis of community input and factored into both risk assessment and remedy selection (E. Livingston-Behan, Department of Energy, personal communication, June 19, 1995).

INCENTIVES, METRICS, AND ACCOUNTABILITY

Like most federal agencies that do not face the market discipline that motivates private organizations, the Department and its contractors have only weak incentives for improved performance. Indeed, in a perverse way to the extent that budgets are allocated according to the magnitude and seriousness of the environmental problems faced by a site, liabilities become an asset. Likewise, with budgets tied to continuing containment and remediation processes, there is not as strong an incentive to complete projects as quickly as might be desired. Some even argue that the present structure of incentives rewards failure. An effort to improve incentives, metrics and accountability for federal employees and contractors would be the most effective way to improve the performance of the Environmental Management Program in meeting its goals, lowering its costs, and improving its safety in the short-term (see also pp. 147–149).

Disincentives within the Environmental Management Program must also be identified and eliminated so that environmental management goals and objectives can be reached. Internal operations and the integration of science, technology and engineering into the implementation of the goals of the Environmental Management Program are hampered by conflicting incentives that are unstated but understood by employees (see also pp. 74–75, 141–142). For instance, although instructed that projects need to be completed within specified periods, employees know from experience that the termination of a project can result in decreased funding for the program. Therefore, they might be led to preserve the program by failing to pursue means to accelerate the cleanup. It is necessary for the unstated goals to be recognized and incentives changed to support the stated goals of the organization; otherwise, employees will have conflicting incentives that undermine management objectives.

Another fundamental disincentive within the Department is that programmatic groups (e.g., those related to defense programs and fossil energy) do not budget for the management and disposal of the wastes that they generate (see also p. 107–108). The Environmental Management Program provides the service and funding for their wastes. Having the various programs of the Department "pay" Environmental Management for the services would provide an incentive for the programmatic groups to minimize waste and use appropriate technology.

The poor incentive structure within the Department carried over to its major contracts until very recently. The Department is to be commended for moving toward performance-based contracts. More should and can be done. Well-defined, carefully negotiated performance contracts can be expected to be much more cost-effective than cost-plus contracts. That change in contract administration should move Environmental Management toward managing its contractors by measuring their performance against desired outcomes, rather than by micromanaging their daily activities (see also p. 103, 153–154). The cost of remediation at Department facilities should be compared with similar activities in private industry and at other government agencies, such as the Department of Defense, to elucidate those differences in management (e.g., the creation of incentives) and procurement that might improve the Department's performance if they were adopted. Training of Department employees will be necessary to give them the skills needed for this new approach to contractor relations, as will a clear statement by Department leadership as to their expectations of the nature of that relationship (see also p. 144).

Environmental Management has recently tried an experiment in "privatization" of the vitrification of high-level nuclear waste at Hanford (see also p. 153). The effort is intended to place greater emphasis on performance by having the contractor bear even greater financial risk in case of failure to meet deadlines and regulatory compliance and to reap rewards for superior performance. There may be reluctance on the part of some states and localities to place as much faith in this new management approach as the Department. For example, while supporting the use of private companies to run the vitrification operation at Hanford, the Washington Department of Ecology and the citizen's Hanford Advisory Board believe this new initiative is too prone to failure and have urged the Department to be prepared to go more slowly and build the plant with Federal funds. It is too early to tell who is correct and if the marketplace will finance private companies to undertake tasks such as the vitrification of wastes at Hanford. If the opposition to new approaches such as privatization is based on the pursuit of unstated goals like providing continued employment and funding for a site, mechanisms should be found to create incentives for states and other stakeholders to willingly participate in these new management approaches.

In general, the Department's Environmental Management Program should use private-sector models and privatization to meet its objective. However, the models must be carefully adapted to suit the public-sector mandates. For instance, if privatization is selected by Environmental Management to accomplish its goals, the Department must recognize that it might have to supply mechanisms to encourage contractors to participate in this privatization, for example, guaranteeing a stream of revenue or allowing customers other than the Department to do business with the selected contractor. Environmental Management might have to create mechanisms to be responsive to the public, which might not release the government from responsibility for carrying out its mandates, regardless of contractual relationships. The Department should not lose sight of the fact that citizens will always hold it, not its contractors, as the party that bears the ultimate responsibility for its activities. That does not have to lead to micromanagement; it might require clearer performance standards or different contractual terms that do not depend on normal contractual remedies for breach of contract.

It is commonly said that civil-service regulations prohibit promotions in the absence of additional supervisory responsibilities and that it is difficult to remove people for poor performance and to reward people for good performance. It is possible to create a civil-service program that provides more incentives for performance (see also p. 148). Pilot programs of up to 5 years can be initiated by government agencies or other units. Environmental Management could implement a different promotion, reward, and firing pilot program. Programs could be modeled after successful industry and utility models. The use of teams for projects can supplement the normal organizational structure. The Department needs more technically knowledgeable people, including people trained in the field of public health, who are able to judge contractors' cost estimates within the context of the objectives set for the contract (see also p. 144). In industry, input by a multifunctional team consisting of a technical project leader, a lawyer, a finance manager, a corporate researcher, and government-relations, real-estate, and construction people starts at the beginning of a project and can continue through completion; the leadership of the team changes as needs change (see also p. 156). Teams are most effective if there has been training and awareness has been raised throughout the entire organization.

As the Department goes to more performance-based contracting, the lines of authority in the field will become blurred compared with the previous practice of cost-reimbursal contracting through field offices. All contracts let by Environmental Management should be administered by Environmental Management. Currently, there is a dysfunctional management loop in which goals are set by one manager (i.e., the Office of Waste Management which reports to the Under Secretary of Energy) and the responsibility for seeing that they are met rests in a different manager (i.e., the Associate Deputy Secretary for Field Management who reports to the Deputy Secretary) who has no direct input to the goal-setting process. Experience shows that control of all aspects of an operating contract under one line of management for its duration is much more effective than administration by multiple parallel lines of management (see also pp. 139–141). Using performance contracts should require fewer Department personnel during the operating phase than are currently employed.

Key to achieving changes in the operation of the Department's Environmental Management Program will be clear leadership from the Secretary. Secretary O'Leary has demonstrated leadership in taking actions to improve stakeholder involvement in the Program. She needs to continue that leadership and actively participate in the fundamental activities related to goal setting and improving the Department's performance as a regulated entity. She must also empower Department staff making cross-program decisions, and take a visible leadership role in decisions that require coordination with other departments, interagency forums, or the President.

GOALS AND PRIORITIES

Establishing a System for Setting Priorities

Any priority-setting system and its attendant tools must be placed in an overall organizational framework to be effective.

Congress usually specifies the *mission* for an agency in the legislation that define its programs and activities. In the case of the Department it has several missions as previously discussed and environmental management is integral to them all.

The *vision* provided by senior managers within the Administration and the Agency gives the agency, its staff, and the public an integrated look at the organization's future state. What does the agency want to accomplish? How does it want to view itself? How does it want the public to view it?

The *goals* are more specific targets for components within the vision, i.e., what specifically is the organization trying to achieve in the short and long term? For example, is Environmental Management trying to maximize the amount of Departmental land that will be available for public use? Is Environmental Management trying to contain waste/contamination and restrict land use to the maximum possible extent to minimize costs? Is Environmental Management going to have a comprehensive technology development program to reduce costs for waste management and environmental restoration activities? Goals are usually set after a dialogue between senior managers of an Agency who have helped formulate the vision and these within the agency who will have direct operational responsibility for accomplishing the goals. In the case of the Environmental Management Program the inclusion of stakeholders in this dialogue is essential.

Objectives are a series of more specific, short term, and quantifiable measures of accomplishment in pursuit of the agency's goals, missions, and vision. Goals may pertain to many facilities or activities, objectives will often pertain to single facilities or activities. Objectives provide answers to questions such as: What parts of each installation will be cleaned up with the intent of release to public use? What types of wastes will be accepted for storage or treatment at each installation? What will be the role of repositories as part of the long-range management of risks? Where will they be sited, what volumes of waste will they be able to accommodate, and in what order will they be received? What areas of the current complex will retain long-term access restrictions? What types of risks will be managed through long-term Department stewardship rather than complete remediation? Objectives are often set after a dialogue between managers of operations at specific Department sites and those who are responsible for achieving the goals. Again, the inclusion of local stakeholders in this process is critical to its success.

These are the main components of a coherent priority-setting system. However, their definition, no matter how rigorously accomplished, will not ensure that the system is effective or useful. This will require that at least as much attention be given to the following steps which are discussed in more detail under the section on implementation below.

The success of a priority-setting system ultimately depends upon how well it is actually *implemented*. For example, will the vision be achieved by Environmental Management dismantling all or selected Department production facilities? Should Environmental Management establish regional waste repositories for ultimate disposal of certain wastes? Should Environmental Management target technology development activities at the most costly and/or longer-term needs?

The Department needs to develop performance standards and metrics to measure as quantitatively as possible its performance and progress. How well does the organization perform and are its activities leading it to its goals? For example, what volume of waste material has been moved to a regional repository? What volume of waste has been adequately characterized? What cleanup levels have been established for contaminated materials on public lands? What is the quantity of land area available for public use? What is the level of potential exposure to Environmental Management's wastes?

The data on the extent of contamination that has been characterized to date are incomplete. Weighting factors are subjectively selected. Calculated probabilities and consequences are of limited defensibility. But none of these facts should be allowed to deter Environmental Management from the obligation to make decisions based on the knowledge, data and evidence at hand. The system should identify these limitations overtly. The presumption is that stakeholders will be receptive to such limitations and act on behalf of the national good.

Need for More-Specific Goals

The Environmental Management Program appears to understand its mission, and this is becoming apparent to the outside world. The Department needs to set specific goals as it asserts leadership in creating the environment to reach those goals. These goals include target cleanup levels, magnitudes of occupational risk to be tolerated, end uses of former Department facilities, and the role of repositories in the overall program. Processes already under way are intended to set many of the needed goals. However, these processes for establishing goals must be resolved as a *precondition* to developing a coherent approach to cleanup. This approach should allow priorities to be set, allow an effective cost-management culture to evolve, and allow decentralization of risk-management decisions back to the individual sites, where existing knowledge is sufficient to support sound decisions. Only when the Department is able to set clear and substantive goals unequivocally will it be able to spend money wisely to manage risks to workers, the public, and the environment and to instill confidence in the public and Congress. However, as further information is developed it may be that some of the goals are unattainable at a cost, risk, or social impact that society is willing to tolerate.

Some goals of the Environmental Management Program are unstated and sometimes conflict with stated goals. That has complicated and slowed the Department's efforts to achieve its long-term objectives for reducing risks for the public, workers, and the environment. For example, the stated goal of the Hanford cleanup is to reduce risk at the site in a timely and efficient manner. However, an unstated goal (except in casual conversation) is to provide continued employment and funding for the site. Organizational structures and decision-making by contractors and Environmental Management employees that would accelerate remediation or reduce the number of people required to carry it out might result in reduced employment or funding. Under the current system, states and local governments want to see rapid action toward achieving safer sites and safer operation, but they also want maximal employment at the Department's sites. Similarly, labor unions and contractors perceive a parochial benefit from larger and slower programs.

Attributes of a Priority-Setting System

A priority-setting system for Environmental Management should have the following attributes:

• *Consistency*. To be successful, the system must be used for a number of years. If it is good, future administrations will accept it; if not, it will be discarded. Congress has a key role in allowing the system to have some permanence. Different levels of funding will dictate different strategies for cleanup, which in turn can affect costs. For example, a budget that allows only containment and facility maintenance necessarily permits only urgent risks to be addressed. Projects that are expensive but smaller risks must continue in the Department inventory until urgent risks (some of which, like the Hanford high-level nuclear waste-tanks, will take considerable time to address) are resolved. The cost of monitoring and maintaining the less-risky sites remains high. At some higher level of funding, the strategy could change to include an aggressive effort to reduce these costs by removing lower-risk sites from the Department inventory as quickly as possible while the most-serious imminent risks continue to be addressed. The longer-term costs might be substantially reduced. If there is no predictability in funding, there can be no priority-setting system that implements a long-term strategy aimed at the highest possible cost-effectiveness.

• *Coherence throughout the Department's complex.* The priority-setting system must be coherent by being functional across the various Department sites and throughout the various elements of the Environmental Management Program. For example, the system must function in setting priorities within the portfolio of facilities that need decontamination and decommissioning just as it must function in determining whether the consolidation of storage sites for plutonium should have higher priority than decontamination and decommissioning of those facilities.

• *Feedback for evolutionary system.* The use of priority-setting tools within the priority-setting system (e.g., the Environmental Restoration Priority-Setting System and the Laboratory Integration and Prioritization System) should be evaluated regularly. Environmental Management generally needs to do more ex post analysis to improve its decision making. Such processes encourage accountability of the Department's managers and contractors.

• *Clarity and transparency.* The goals and workings of the process should be clear to all participants and encourage the exchange of concerns to foster common conclusions. The methodology to quantify funding decisions must not have a hidden agenda.

• *Participation of stakeholders.* The legacy of low public trust and credibility of the Department was based, in the past, on the need for secrecy in some programs. The Secretary has taken steps to involve people affected by the Department's actions in the decision-making process. That has been successful and should be continued formally. Although stakeholders do not have authority to determine funding, they should participate in and understand the basis of, funding decisions. The inclusion of Indian Nation, state, and local stakeholders in this process for fiscal 1997 is laudable.

Risk Assessment and Cost-Benefit Analysis

We recognize that Environmental Management, in response to a Congressional request, recently produced a preliminary evaluation of the risk of the many activities and facilities in the Environmental Management complex (DOE, 1995d). However, as its title suggests, this is only a first step.

Environmental Management should continue to develop a risk-based approach by having risk assessment done as one of the major activities under the Environmental Management umbrella. That is especially useful when priorities must be set and decisions about worker, public, and environmental health must be balanced against each other and against costs. The process should be open so that the results will be understood by both the Department and stakeholders. It should undergo extensive peer review by outside panels. The assessments, which will take several iterations to perfect, should compare the risks at the several major sites to enable prudent allocation of resources and to decide which sites should be approached first (NRC, 1994).

Ultimately, the process should be able to identify the locations and situations that pose the most serious risks to the public, to workers at Department sites, and to the environment. Imminent risks should have the highest priority for action. For nonimminent risks, risk assessment should identify the benefits of risk reduction as part of overall cost-benefit analyses, which should form the basis for further priority-setting and resolution of contamination problems that must be addressed as required by law or compliance agreements.

A cautionary note on the use of risk assessment, cost-benefit analysis, and other tools used in priority-setting is necessary. These tools are just that, tools for the manager and stakeholders to use in the decision-making process. They are only as good as the information that is used in performing the analysis and ultimately, there are many factors which might affect the decision-maker outside of these data-driven tools.

SCIENCE AND TECHNOLOGY

Science and technology play key roles in virtually all activities of Environmental Management. They help to determine priorities for site cleanup by providing a basis for sound risk assessments and provide the tools for reaching remediation goals and priorities and ensuring that actions of the Department are the best that can be done. For environmental management problems that lack good solutions, Environmental Management needs an effective way to bring Department and other scientific and technical resources to bear. The Department must dramatically improve its research and technology-development outreach. That can be accomplished only by widely opening the Department's research and development program to all qualified professionals and organizations, regardless of type or location (including international expertise). Concomitantly with opening the Environmental Management R&D procurement system, a broad-based system of external peer review must be carefully implemented and monitored to ensure that the best proposals are selected.

Focus Areas

Environmental Management has designated five priority or Focus Areas for technology development. The purpose of the focused approach is to bring together users and developers to decrease cost, decrease risk, and develop ways to do what cannot be done today. In addition, a number of cross-cutting or common subjects have been identified by the Department for special attention: characterization, monitoring, and sensors; efficient separation and processing; robotics; and technology transfer.

Keys to the success of the Department's technology development process are that it be intimately linked with identified customer needs (i.e., the site-specific application of the technology) and that it use quantitative tools, such as risk analysis and cost-benefit analysis. The process of technology selection must also be iterative so that technologies under development reflect recent advances. The committee believes that the Focus Areas that have been defined provide an appropriate structure for using these approaches. However, we are concerned that implementation of the focus approach has fallen short of the intended mark primarily because users, researchers, and developers have not yet been fully integrated into the decision-making process for selecting new technologies. We recommend that steps be taken to ensure that user involvement in the focus approach is substantial enough (and has sufficient expertise) to affect the early selection and continued refinement of technologies for development.

National Laboratories, Universities, and Industry: Partnerships and Competition

The decision as to whether National Laboratories, universities, or industry should take the lead in a basic-research effort or in the development of any particular technology should be based on a competitive process that undergoes external review, not on formula or some other form of entitlement. Teaming together and partnering these different groups is often the most-effective approach.

National Laboratories constitute an extraordinary technical resource both in capability and in size. It must be recognized, however, that the Laboratories are unique in culture and expertise (especially with nuclear materials), which can be both an advantage and a disadvantage in bringing new technologies and science to bear in Environmental Management's activities. There must be strong external benchmarking and extensive peer review of research and technology-development efforts in the National Laboratories. The Laboratories must also be open to procurement of outside capabilities even when the main body of the R&D takes place inside. As with all participants in the technology-development effort, the Laboratories should structure efforts to be responsive to the technology needs of customers.

Experience has demonstrated time and time again that the National Laboratories are most effective at producing technologies that have potential for commercialization if they are linked to industry at the earliest possible time. The idea is for industry to provide "technology pull" that can guide the R&D so that the product meets customer requirements and there are no surprises when the technology is turned over to industry for commercialization.

REGULATORY MEASURES

External Regulation

The Department is subject to external regulation and in some particulars is self-regulating (see also p. 34). There is an inherent tension (many would say a conflict of interest) between meeting primary mission requirements (e.g., dismantlement of the nuclear weapons arsenal) and ensuring adequate protection of worker safety, public safety, and environmental concerns. Because of that tension, regulatory systems in which the entities regulate themselves lack credibility. Given the magnitude of the risks associated with manufacturing and in maintaining and dismantling the nuclear weapons stockpile, effective and credible external regulatory programs are necessary. We believe that the Department's self-regulation of its nuclear-related activities should be eliminated. We are not prepared to recommend an appropriate successor agency for the Department's current regulatory roles, but clearly one would be needed. This Subcommittee is aware that any transition from self-regulation to external regulation will be difficult in view of the very specialized and complicated issues which the Department faces. This transition should be done cautiously and carefully.

Overcoming Regulatory "Obstacles"—Using Existing Flexibility

In a number of instances in which the Department and its contractors cite regulatory restrictions as prohibiting common sense and safe solutions to their problems, there is usually some form of regulatory flexibility that has not been applied. The Department should increase the use of the flexibility that is available in the regulations (see also pp. 35, 111–112). Obtaining variances, waivers, or their functional equivalents in threshold standards, treatment requirements, and groundwater monitoring are examples of such flexibility. Industry often works with regulators to find mutually acceptable compromises in the face of regulatory restrictions. The Department should encourage Environmental Management and its contractors to use the available flexibility. The focus of the Department and its employees should be on achieving long-term goals, not on meeting the detailed schedules of current compliance agreements where they are in conflict with these goals. In cases where these conflicts arise and remediation is impeded, the Department should seek to renegotiate the compliance agreement.

Streamlining Regulatory Measures

The current regulatory system is a confusing patchwork assembled, at least in part, with weapons production in mind (see also p. 47). A number of potential problems are caused when the authorities of multiple regulators, such as states, the Defense Nuclear Facilities Safety Board, and the Environmental Protection Agency (and sometimes the Department), for cleanup of a given site or operable unit overlap. The problems include the following:

• When there is lack of agreement among multiple regulators, regulatory compliance is slowed to attain a consistent decision.

• Additional resources are expended in coordination.

• Differences between the objectives of multiple regulations inhibit priority-setting.

Lead Regulator

If more than one regulatory entity, including state and federal agencies, has jurisdiction over a Department site, a lead regulator should be designated for a cleanup activity or group of cleanup activities and every effort should be made to have as few different regulators at a site as possible (see also pp. 37–39). The lead regulator should oversee all day-to-day compliance or cleanup actions and decisions and should resolve disputes. Other regulators on a site should recognize and defer to the authority of the lead agency. The mechanism for achieving this goal could be its incorporation into existing compliance agreements.

Other measures that would streamline the regulatory process for Environmental Management include

• Early involvement between the Department, its regulators, and other stakeholders in scoping out projects and budgets for compliance agreements.

• Permission for site cleanups to occur under RCRA closure or corrective action in lieu of CERCLA where both RCRA and CERCLA are applicable.

• Encouragement of use of the "one document" approach to satisfy RCRA and CERCLA.

• The functional equivalence of RCRA to NEPA where RCRA applies, as NEPA and CERCLA have been integrated to be functionally equivalent where CERCLA fulfills NEPA.

• Cross training of regulatory Department, and contractor personnel in applicable laws.

• Delegation of CERCLA to states. There are a number of approaches as to how this could be done. States could be mandated to require exactly what is currently required of those regulated by the federal regulators with jurisdiction over CERCLA or states could be permitted to have more stringent requirements than current federal regulations.

PUBLIC PARTICIPATION: SEARCHING FOR CONSENSUS TO ACHIEVE CREDIBILITY

A Department decision that is supported by sound scientific and technical understanding will not necessarily lead to a successful result. High-quality scientific and technical information is of little value in decision-making if it is not understood and accepted by stakeholders. The challenge for Environmental Management managers is to bring together a variety of factors into a well-balanced, implementable decision. The call for all Departmental efforts to be open and transparent to stakeholders recurred throughout the work of this committee's four subcommittees. Whether the issue is the decision process for technology selection or the performance of a risk assessment for remedial-action options, involving stakeholders is crucial for creating workable consensus. The Department operates in a political environment in which citizen support is essential to avoid costly and protracted litigation or similar consequences. Consensus is the key to credibility in this political environment. Without credibility, little will be accomplished by Environmental Management in reaching its vision or in completing its mission.

References

Blush, Steven M. and Thomas H. Heitman. 1995. Train Wreck Along the River of Money: An Evaluation of the Hanford Cleanup, A Report for the U.S. Senate Committee on Energy and Natural Resources, Washington, D.C.

Consortium for Environmental Risk Evaluation. Health and Ecological Risks at the U.S. Department of Energy's Nuclear Weapons Complex: A Qualitative Evaluation. CERE Interim Risk Report. March 1995.

DOE (U.S. Department of Energy). 1995a. Closing the Circle on the Splitting of the Atom: The Environmental Legacy of Nuclear Weapons Production in the United States and What the Department of Energy is Doing About It. The U.S. Department of Energy, Office of Environmental Management, Office of Strategic Planning and Analysis (EM-4), Washington, D.C.

DOE (U.S. Department of Energy). 1995b. Estimating the Cold War Mortgage: The 1995 Baseline Environmental Management Report, Volume I, March 1995. U.S. Department of Energy, Office of Environmental Management, Washington, D.C.

DOE (U.S. Department of Energy). 1995c. Environmental Management 1995: Progress and Plans of the Environmental Management Program. The U.S. Department of Energy, Office of Environmental Management, Washington, D.C.

DOE (U.S. Department of Energy). 1995d. Risks and the Risk Debate: Searching for Common Ground "The First Step". The U.S. Department of Energy, Office of Environmental Management, Washington, D.C.

NRC (National Research Council). 1994. Building Consensus Through Risk Assessment and Risk Management in the Department of Energy's Environmental Remediation Program. National Academy Press, Washington, D.C.

NRC (National Research Council). 1995. Technical Bases for Yucca Mountain Standards. National Academy Press, Washington, D.C.

OTA (U.S. Congress, Office of Technology Assessment). 1991. Complex Cleanup: The Environmental Legacy of Nuclear Weapons Production. OTA-O484. U.S. Government Printing Office, Washington, D.C.

Part II
Evaluation of
Regulatory Measures

SUBCOMMITTEE ON EVALUATION OF
REGULATORY MEASURES

DON CLAY (*Chair*), President, Don Clay Associates, Inc.
ANDREW P. CAPUTO, Attorney, Natural Resources Defense Council
JAMES R. CURTISS, Attorney, Winston & Strawn
MARSHALL E. DRUMMOND, President, Eastern Washington University
DANIEL S. MILLER, First Assistant Attorney General, Colorado
Department of Law
BERNARD J. REILLY, Corporate Council, DuPont Legal
MARY RIVELAND, Director, Washington State Department of Ecology

Staff

Ray Wassel, Senior Program Officer
Ruth Danoff, Project Assistant

Introduction

This is the report of the Subcommittee on the Evaluation of Regulatory Measures. Biographical information on the members is provided in the appendix. The letter from Mr. Grumbly, mentioned above, indicates that this subcommittee's work should examine how the performance of the Environmental Management Program could be improved through regulatory measures, such as new statutes, revised statutes, and revised regulatory agreements.

Our workshop was held on June 19–20, 1995, in Washington, D.C. The workshop agenda and list of participants are included in the appendix. We heard presentations from representatives of DOE headquarters, DOE sites, contractors at DOE sites, Environmental Protection Agency (EPA) headquarters and EPA regions, the Nuclear Regulatory Commission, state attorneys general, state environmental agencies, and others. A roundtable discussion was held after the formal presentations to explore some of the relevant issues further. The participants identified what they considered to be the most important matters to address. We used the results of the roundtable discussion as a springboard in developing a framework for this report and for identifying important issues that we might address.

DOE's environmental restoration activities must be conducted pursuant to applicable environmental laws. The principal environmental laws dictating how the cleanup is to be performed at the weapons sites are the Resource Conservation and Recovery Act, as amended (RCRA), the Comprehensive Environmental Response, Compensation, and Liability Act, as amended (CERCLA) (also known as Superfund), and the Atomic Energy Act of 1954, as amended. Many DOE sites are on the National Priorities List (NPL) developed under CERCLA. The National Environmental Policy Act (NEPA) of 1970 mandates that all federal agencies and departments take into consideration the adverse effects that their actions might have on the environment. NEPA requires that agency actions be reviewed early in the planning process and that the process be open to public participation. DOE's environmental-restoration efforts are also subject to state laws and regulations, including those adopted under the authority of RCRA and CERCLA.

All high-level radioactive waste and most transuranic waste are mixed waste, usually because of the presence of organic solvents or heavy metals, in addition to the radioactive components. The hazardous component of mixed waste is regulated under the RCRA. In 1992, Congress passed the Federal Facility Compliance Act, which amended RCRA to make federal facilities subject to the same fines and penalties as any private corporation if they violate the law. The law also requires DOE to develop plans for mixed-waste treatment, subject to approval of the states or the U.S. Environmental Protection Agency (EPA).

For sites that are required to undergo CERCLA cleanup, DOE is required to enter an agreement with EPA regarding how the cleanup should be carried out. EPA has states join in these compliance agreements. Thus, the agreements are often signed by three parties: DOE, EPA, and the state where the facility is. Compliance agreements are also formed with regard to requirements under RCRA and when both CERCLA and RCRA apply. Compliance agreements must include at least a schedule for accomplishing the cleanup, arrangements for operation and maintenance of the site, and a review of the cleanup options considered and the remedy selected. Such agreements are enforceable by states against DOE facilities, and civil penalties may be imposed for failure or refusal of a facility to comply with a compliance agreement. State enforcement under CERCLA agreements occurs through citizen suits, but states have separate enforcement authorities. Compliance agreements might give additional authority from multiple statutes, and enforcement provisions vary because of the construct of the agreement and the underlying regulations.

Sites that have not been placed on the NPL operate only under the regulatory jurisdiction of RCRA. A major difference between CERCLA and RCRA is that CERCLA coverage includes both hazardous and radioactive contamination, whereas RCRA and its corrective-action provisions cover only hazardous waste and the hazardous portion of mixed waste. Releases of radioactivity to the environment are regulated exclusively by DOE under the authority of the Atomic Energy Act. DOE has its own set of internal directives (DOE orders) governing radioactive-waste management and the limitations of radionuclide releases to the environment. The Atomic Energy Act gives DOE broad authority over radioactive waste with the exception of facilities for the storage and disposal of high-level radioactive waste and spent nuclear fuel, which are regulated by the Nuclear Regulatory Commission. Thus, DOE orders are wide-ranging and include environmental protection, worker safety, project management, facility design, transportation, emergency planning, and personnel. In addition, each DOE contractor independently maintains its own sets of guidance documents and internal procedures to implement these orders.

According to DOE's 1995 Baseline Environmental Management Report, the life-cycle cost estimate for DOE's Environmental Management Program ranges from $200 to $350 billion in constant 1995 dollars, with a midrange estimate of $230 billion. That included not only the $172 billion for dealing with the nuclear-weapons complex legacy, but also $24 billion for future wastes from nuclear-weapons activities and $34 billion for past and future wastes from other activities. The projected cost for treatment, storage, and disposal of waste generated by continuing defense and research activities is $19 billion. The large projected cost for support of future continuing programs indicates the value of vigorous pollution-prevention efforts to reduce costs and threats.

The base-case cost estimate begins in 1995 and ends in about 2070, when environmental-management activities are projected to be substantially completed. The estimate does not include amounts expended since the program's formal inception in October 1989—about $23 billion—or costs incurred before 1989. Nor does it include costs beyond 2070 for long-term surveillance and maintenance, which are estimated at about $50–75 million per year. Those costs are assumed to continue indefinitely after a disposal site or restricted-access area is closed.

DOE's Environmental Management program and regulatory measures have been assessed by a number of organizations. The appendix includes summaries of relevant documents prepared by various organizations and individuals.

Our Approach to Evaluating Regulatory Measures

We focused our deliberations on regulatory statutes, regulations, and their implementation regarding environmental remediation and waste management in DOE's Environmental Management Program. Our emphasis has been on public health. Related issues, such as exposure of workers involved in environmental cleanup, are being addressed by the Advisory Committee on External Regulation of Department of Energy Nuclear Safety. That advisory committee is an independent review panel that will recommend whether and how DOE nuclear facilities and operations might be externally regulated to protect health, safety, and the environment, to eliminate unnecessary oversight, and to reduce costs.

In this report, we first discuss the principles that guided our deliberations. Next, we address regulations within DOE, multiple external regulators, land-use planning, standards for residual risk, and considerations of cost effectiveness and risk. We conclude with what we consider to be our principal recommendations.

We developed the following set of principles to guide our deliberations. We believe that DOE and its regulators should develop a corresponding set. These principles are based upon input from workshop participants and our judgment. Many of the principles are discussed later in the report in the context of relevant conclusions and recommendations.

• Public sites, including those of DOE, and private sites should be treated similarly by regulatory measures, and expected outcomes should be the same where the problems are similar. (However, DOE sites provide an opportunity to demonstrate new technologies that private parties might not want to attempt at private sites.)

• A lead regulator, whether a federal or state agency, would expedite the resolution of regulatory problems. Once the lead is established, flexibility inherent in existing regulations should be used to improve outcomes. Because sites are diverse, it would be inappropriate to develop a one-size-fits-all regulation.

• Because many needs compete for scarce resources, it is essential to strive for cost-effective environmental management for health, safety, and the environment. But protection of health, safety, and the environment must be the paramount consideration that drives DOE's EM activities.

• Interim remedies for contaminated sites, such as land-use controls, should not be considered permanent, because residual risks can be very long-lived. However, when such remedies offer cost-effective means of protecting public health and communities are willing to maintain them, they should be pursued. It is important to continue to seek permanent remedies, but their absence is no excuse for inaction.

• Full dialogue among stakeholders, including state regulators, should be pursued before decision-making.

• Regulatory goals should be adopted on the basis of priorities set through an open, public process that focuses on protecting workers, public health, and the environment. Efforts to meet future milestones should also have this focus. Such an approach can aid in gaining stakeholder acceptance and the development of shared goals between the regulator and the regulated. Therefore, the focus should be on achieving long-term goals, not on meeting the detailed schedules of current compliance agreements. In cases where these conflicts arise and remediation is impeded, the Department should seek to renegotiate the compliance agreement.

• The focus should be on improved implementation of existing regulatory measures; development of new legislation should be considered only secondarily.

Regulation of DOE's Environmental Management Program

From the beginning of the Manhattan Project until after 1970, DOE and its predecessors were not subject to external regulation. Beginning in the 1970s, federal legislation waiving the federal government's sovereign immunity from state and federal environmental laws was enacted. DOE resisted the application of hazardous-waste regulation for several years. That resistance resulted in a 1984 federal court decision (*L.E.A.F. v. Hodel*) rejecting DOE's contention that RCRA did not apply to its activities because it would conflict with the Atomic Energy Act. In 1987, DOE acknowledged that RCRA applied to the hazardous-waste component of mixed radioactive and hazardous wastes.

In the late 1980s, DOE's operations rapidly went from having virtually no oversight to being the subject of multiple internal and external reviews, including a highly publicized criminal investigation at Rocky Flats that resulted in a plea agreement in which DOE's contractor pleaded guilty to 10 criminal counts under 2 federal environmental laws and paid an $18.5 million fine. Such intense scrutiny resulted in a dramatic change in DOE's attitude toward compliance with its own orders and with external regulations. Suddenly, DOE became overconservative, in the bureaucratic sense, in interpreting regulatory requirements. At the same time, it began to place great reliance on its contractors in determining how to comply with regulatory requirements (both externally imposed requirements and DOE orders). Combined with a lack of sufficient properly trained contract managers and the prevailing use of cost-plus contracting mechanisms (which create financial

34

incentives to increase costs of compliance), DOE's overconservative approach has led to substantial inefficiencies and unnecessary costs in complying with environmental-protection and nuclear-safety requirements.

Also in the late 1980s, DOE shut down portions of the nuclear weapons complex until a series of safety and environmental problems could be resolved. While those facilities were shut down, the Cold War ended, and DOE decided that some of them (e.g., those at Hanford and Rocky Flats) would not be reopened. The widespread safety and environmental protection concerns at its facilities prompted DOE to re-examine its policies regarding self-regulation and its approach to external regulators (i.e., state and federal environmental regulators).

DOE AS AN EXTERNALLY REGULATED ENTITY

We found that DOE has experienced considerable difficulty in making the transition from operation in an environment in which it was largely self-regulated to a much more open atmosphere with substantial external oversight. DOE has made substantial progress in becoming more open, but its success in adjusting to external regulation has been uneven, in part because of the events that surrounded the first serious efforts to impose external regulatory requirements on DOE, discussed above.

To its credit, senior management of DOE has recognized the shortcomings in its contracting practices. It has hired many federal employees to provide better contract oversight, and it is rebidding many of its contracts to emphasize cost-effective compliance. As noted below, DOE is also in the process of promulgating its orders as rules and in so doing has established a decision-making process for determining the necessary and sufficient requirements that must be established to comply with the new regulations case by case. Those reforms should help to reduce DOE's costs of environmental protection, worker-safety, and nuclear-safety compliance. DOE's progress in implementing the reforms should be monitored to ensure that it achieves its goals.

However, many state and federal regulators have observed that DOE seems not to know how to "work with" regulators. In particular, outside regulators have repeatedly expressed concerns over DOE's failure to communicate with them in a timely manner regarding compliance matters. That failure inhibits regulators from assisting DOE in complying with regulatory requirements in a common-sense, low-cost fashion, for example, by pointing out overconservative regulatory interpretations. Failure to communicate in a timely fashion might also delay DOE's compliance with regulatory requirements in particular situations.

SELF-REGULATION

We think that the weaknesses of a system of self-regulation are plain: there is an inherent tension (many would say a conflict of interest) between meeting "primary mission" requirements (e.g., rapid buildup of nuclear weapons arsenal) and ensuring adequate protection of worker-safety, nuclear-safety, and environmental concerns. Any regulatory system must rely in part on voluntary efforts to comply, but external enforcement is also necessary to ensure a consistently high compliance. Because of that inherent tension, regulatory systems in which the entity responsible for compliance is also responsible for enforcing compliance lack credibility. Given the magnitude of the risks associated with manufacturing and maintaining the nuclear weapons stockpile, effective and credible regulatory programs are necessary.

We agree that DOE's self-regulation of its nuclear-related activities should be eliminated. Indeed, DOE has established the Advisory Committee on External Regulation of Department of Energy Nuclear Safety to provide advice specifically on how nuclear-related activities at DOE facilities might be regulated.

DOE ORDERS

In addition to the general problems of self-regulation, DOE and others have identified a number of problems with the particular system of "DOE orders" that DOE and its predecessors had developed to implement the requirements of the Atomic Energy Act. The orders were not developed in a coordinated manner and were never promulgated as regulations under the Administrative Procedures Act (APA). They often failed to establish clear requirements, and there was no administrative process for determining how each order should be applied to a particular activity. Consequently, many of the orders were essentially unenforceable and generally were not enforced. Recently, DOE began reviewing its orders, rewriting them, and promulgating them under the APA to address those concerns. We support DOE's process of reviewing its orders and converting them to rules that have a clear legal foundation; this should increase the clarity of obligations placed on contractors and provide a clear mechanism for enforcing obligations. However, conversion of DOE orders to promulgated rules is not an adequate solution to the problems created by self-regulation. The reason is that the purpose of the orders (and of the new regulations) is to increase contractors' accountability to DOE. They do not (and cannot) address the lack of DOE accountability to the public and affected communities by self-regulation.

We also support elimination of orders that are redundant with outside authorities, obsolete because of their focus on the past production mission, or overprescriptive. In addition, DOE should hold its contractors responsible for conducting similar reviews of internal procedures intended to implement DOE orders so as to streamline the entire system.

MULTIPLE REGULATORS

As noted above, we agree that DOE's self-regulation of its nuclear-related activities should be eliminated, it is necessary to make a transition to external regulation, and we are not making specific recommendations regarding who should assume the responsibility for such external regulation. However, we note that the manner in which external environmental regulation has been implemented has contributed to the creation of multiple regulators and overlapping regulatory requirements for some activities, including management of mixed radioactive and hazardous wastes. If done poorly, moving to external regulation of nuclear safety could complicate this situation. There is some degree of communication between entities with overlapping responsibilities (DOE and the Defense Nuclear Safety Board on the one hand, and state and EPA hazardous-waste regulators on the other), but no formal mechanisms have been developed to coordinate implementation of these regulatory systems. In providing for external regulation of DOE nuclear safety, care should be taken to ensure coordination with hazardous-waste and related regulatory programs, particularly with respect to mixed waste.

In our view, external regulation would give public credibility to DOE and hence facilitate efforts to move forward with the EM mission. However, the current regulatory system is a confusing patchwork assembled, at least in part, with weapons production in mind. A number of potential problems are caused when the authorities of multiple regulators, such as states and EPA (and sometimes DOE), overlap for cleanup of the same site or operable unit. For example:

• When there is lack of agreement among multiple regulators, regulatory compliance is slowed to attain a consistent decision.
• Additional resources are expended in coordination.
• The presence of different objectives of multiple regulations inhibits priority-setting.

CURRENT ACTIVITIES

Several isolated efforts are under way to address the problem of multiple regulators. Such efforts include:

• An effort sponsored by EPA and DOE to increase consistency of cleanups performed under RCRA and CERCLA and to provide better integration of the two statutes.
• State agreements with EPA in dividing the workload at the Hanford facility to strive for a single regulator on one project.
• DOE review of orders from headquarters.
• The Hazardous Waste Identification Rule, proposed by EPA, which is

intended to provide exemptions from RCRA Subtitle C waste-management requirements for low-toxicity hazardous wastes that are managed in a way that is protective of human health and the environment and which includes consideration of mixed radiologic and RCRA hazardous waste (mixed waste).

• The Corrective Action Management Unit Rule (an RCRA regulation), promulgated by EPA and adopted by a number of states, which allows more site-specific, tailored management of cleanup wastes than had been the case under RCRA (for example not requiring compliance with "land-disposal restriction" treatment requirements and not requiring that remediation wastes be placed in a landfill that meets RCRA's "minimum technological requirements."

• DOE's suggestion to Congress (in response to the Speaker's Task Force on Nuclear Cleanup and Tritium Production (1995) referred to as "turbocharge") that a national policy be set for streamlining the cleanup requirements of RCRA and CERCLA, including several specific options.

—Dividing the workload between regulatory agencies and setting out a unified approach to meeting RCRA and CERCLA requirements.

—Prohibiting states from exercising RCRA corrective action authority at federal sites on the National Priorities List (NPL).

—Requiring EPA to remove a federal site or operable unit from the NPL if a state imposes corrective-action requirements at the same facility or operable unit.

POSSIBLE COMPREHENSIVE SOLUTIONS

We recommend the following solutions for problems caused when the authorities of multiple regulators overlap for the cleanup of the same site or operable unit. Some of the solutions would involve administrative changes in how existing laws are implemented. Other solutions would require statutory changes.

• Increase use of flexibility currently available in the regulations, e.g., obtaining variances, waivers, or their functional equivalents in threshold standards, treatment requirements, and groundwater monitoring.

• Designate a lead regulator for each cleanup activity or group of cleanup activities. The lead regulator would oversee all day-to-day actions and decisions and resolve disputes. Other regulators on site would recognize the authority of the lead agency and defer to it.

• Involve DOE, its regulators, and other stakeholders early in scoping out projects and budget for compliance agreements.

• Allow site cleanups to occur under RCRA closure or corrective action in lieu of CERCLA when both RCRA and CERCLA are applicable.

• Encourage use of "one-document" approach to satisfy RCRA and CERCLA.

• Just as NEPA and CERCLA have been integrated to be functionally equivalent where CERCLA fulfills NEPA, make RCRA, where it applies, fulfill the requirements of NEPA.

• Cross train regulators, DOE, and contractor personnel in multiple laws.

• Allow CERCLA to be delegated to states by requiring them to follow exactly what is required in CERCLA or allow states to have their own cleanup program, which might or might not be allowed to be more stringent than federal requirements when regulatory authority is delegated to states, mechanisms would be needed to ensure that they are adequately and cost-effectively performing their regulatory function.

Responsible Stewardship

We have taken as a guiding principle that lack of appropriate technology or a permanent solution for remediating a polluted site or facility should not be an excuse for taking no appropriate steps on a near-term or interim basis and is not an excuse for inaction. Responsible stewardship means furthering protection of the public and the environment by undertaking near-term or midterm action to remediate a site when no permanent solution exists. Communities and states that are willing to make institutional commitments to implementing plans for near-term and midterm remedies are participating in responsible stewardship. In the absence of permanent solutions, responsible stewardship is desirable because it allows progress to be made by providing adequate protection against environmental and human-health risks that are serious and long-lived. It deals with waste in relatively short periods, say, 20 years. After such a period, existing approaches should be re-examined, and society can decide what to do with site cleanup for the next 20 years. Until permanent solutions are developed, irreversible actions should be avoided. Furthermore, the benefits of actions considered over the short term should not obscure the benefits of long-term solutions. If many 20-year periods are considered together, the costs of taking only the short-term view could be huge.

Decisions about contamination along the Columbia River at Hanford illustrate the idea of responsible stewardship. Stakeholders have placed a high priority on unrestricted access to lands along the river. Stakeholders have also acknowledged that no near-term solution exists for complete remediation of the underlying groundwater. So work has focused on the remediation of soils and on remediating and containing sources of groundwater contamination while retaining the long-term goal of unrestricted use of the groundwater.

Another example is the management of transuranic waste at the Idaho National Engineering Laboratory. Recently, DOE has undertaken a major effort at consolidating, repackaging, monitoring, and sheltering its transuranic waste. Instead of being exposed to the effects of weather and the risk of corrosion and leaks, drums containing transuranic waste are stored on concrete or asphalt pads under weather-resistant structures. Much of the waste had been stored in earth-covered berms, which were expected to be needed for only a few years, until a permanent disposal site became available. DOE is now repacking drums that began to corrode or leak and is building new interim storage facilities (DOE, 1995a).

Responsible stewardship should not be relied on to provide permanent solutions. Some components of radioactive waste can continue to be a threat to human health and safety for thousands of years or more. A National Research Council report (NRC, 1995) concludes, for high-level nuclear-waste disposal, that although it might be reasonable to assume that a system of interim safeguards can be relied on for some period, there is no scientific basis for assuming the long-term effectiveness of institutional controls to protect against releases of the stored radioactive materials.

Land-Use Planning

Many contaminated sites and facilities could be restored to a pristine condition, suitable for any desired use; or they could be restored to a point where they pose no health risks for some uses (e.g., industrial development or recreation). In other cases when permanent remedies are unavailable, the surrounding communities could be protected for the near future by fencing off the sites and facilities. Each of those options is associated with its own set of costs and benefits. Land-use decisions like these are relevant to the consideration of regulatory measures in that different cleanup-level goals might be set for different land-use options with little or no difference in risks to human health.

DOE believes that current efforts at land-use planning and the mechanisms for their implementation are inadequate. In cases not bound by legal obligations or commitments by DOE, future land use is unclear. DOE has begun working with stakeholders and regulators regarding the ultimate disposition of lands currently managed by DOE (DOE, 1995b).

We believe that land use and groundwater impact should be among the first considerations in planning remediation. Furthermore, there is a need for a formal decision framework for future land-use and cleanup standards. The framework must include an opportunity for input from all interested parties including Indian Nations and other affected communities. It would be used to develop enforceable but modifiable agreements.

If land-use restrictions are to be incorporated in cleanup remedies for DOE sites, there must be clear assurance that the land use will be controlled for the duration of the contamination. This is a serious problem for sites contaminated with long-lived radionuclides. The record of decisions in selecting the remedy should incorporate specific commitments by DOE designed to maintain the necessary institutional controls over the lifetime of the contamination. Where contaminants are so long-lived that such commitments are impossible, the remedy should include specific procedures designed to reassess regularly the adequacy of the institutional controls and, where such reassessment detects problems, either to address the inadequacies or to reopen the remedy.

DOE is extending the CERCLA-based EPA land-use directive (issued on May 25, 1995) to RCRA corrective action so that reasonably anticipated future land use is identified early in the decision-making process on the basis of using community input, in both risk assessment and remedy selection (E. Livingston-Behan, DOE, personal communication, June 19, 1995).

A National Research Council report (NRC, 1994) recommends that three levels of site remediation be considered with respect to risk (imminent and long-term) and cost as part of a process for setting remedial-action priorities for contaminated sites. The three levels are sufficient remediation to contain contaminants so that they would not present substantial risk to human health and the environment, restoration of a site to the point where no land-use restrictions would be necessary, and restoration to return the site to precontamination quality. Such consideration would allow sound judgments to be made concerning the degree of cleanup that should be pursued at a given site. It would indicate when more extensive cleanup at a site might not involve substantially more cost than containment.

Residual-Risk Regulation and National Cleanup Standards

Although the general goal of environmental restoration is cleanup, there is no universal answer to the question "How clean is clean enough?". Cleanup under CERCLA is considered complete if federal and state cleanup standards are met. Standards exist for drinking-water supplies (protection of human health) and surface waters (protection of ecosystems). Few such standards exist for soils, even with respect to hazardous chemicals, and no standards have been designed specifically for cleanup of most radionuclides in soil. The only standards designed for the cleanup of radionuclides are those for land and buildings contaminated by uranium-mill tailings at inactive uranium-processing sites.

Under CERCLA, risk assessments are conducted to determine the relationship between contaminant concentrations at an affected site and the likelihood of adverse effects on human health and the environment. Cleanup levels are established by calculating the expected lifetime cancer risk from the risk estimates, as well as by compliance with applicable or relevant and appropriate requirements (ARARs).

In an effort to remedy the lack of consistent radiation-cleanup standards, the EPA and the Nuclear Regulatory Commission are developing the Radiation Site Cleanup Regulation (40 CFR 196) and Radiological Criteria for Decommissioning (10 CFR 20), respectively. These requirements will apply to DOE sites. An EPA and Nuclear Regulatory Commission memorandum of understanding (57 FR 54127) discusses how the two agencies' parallel approach will yield regulations that are consistent, are protective of public health and the environment, and are issued in a timely manner.

There needs to be a standard framework for acceptable risk vis-a-vis land-use and water-use categories that gives stakeholders leeway within a fixed range of permissible risk. Such a framework would be used as a point of departure for site-specific considerations. It would permit flexibility for cleanup above or below the standard. Decisions would be made with the understanding that new knowledge (concerning toxicity, migration, or innovative technology) could trigger revisiting of cleanup plans.

Cost Effectiveness and Risk Considerations

Resources are scarce and contested, so advocated solutions should be well justified regarding cost and should be related to risk. It is most useful to consider cost effectiveness and risk at the macroscopic level to identify points of gross disparity among site-cleanup efforts. Such a consideration would be one of several tools in making decisions. Other tools are considerations of land use and cultural, social, and economic factors. The benefits of a remedy that is selected as protective, practical within time and technical grounds, and acceptable to the affected community should bear a reasonable relation to its cost. It would be very time- and resource-consuming to justify cost and risk-benefit relationship in an elaborate, quantitative way. Given the many assumptions required for such an analysis and the resulting uncertainties, it would be infeasible to establish that a particular course of action is the least-cost alternative.

Overall Findings and Recommendations

STREAMLINING THE REGULATORY PROCESS

In most instances, difficulties arising from the overlap of regulations are due not to the statutes as written, but to differences in how the standards are implemented and in the numerous parties involved in their application. With the specific exceptions noted in this report, legislative changes are not necessary for DOE to move forward with an effective, efficient cleanup. The department should focus its attention on the administrative and organizational changes noted in this report, which are likely to pay off in a better program.

Regulators need one of them to be in the lead and to be a spokesperson and need to rely on flexibility in the current regulations. However, streamlining efforts must be handled carefully to avoid cutting people out of the process. Streamlining should be used not as a means of vitiating regulatory measures, but as a means of facilitating their implementation and compliance.

Streamlining compliance agreements is especially important. In some cases, such agreements tend to be too prescriptive. Milestones are set at every step and add too much cost for the incremental environmental value. A rigorous schedule makes it difficult to accommodate budget realities. However, in the absence of milestones or with excessive flexibility (e.g., 5 years or more) for meeting them, it is possible that no real progress would be made.

Milestones in cleanup agreements should focus on major outcomes or results and allow for flexibility in reaching them. The milestones should be performance-based and adjustable where appropriate.

RESPONSIBLE STEWARDSHIP

Responsible stewardship, as discussed above, is a reasonable way to address the cleanup problem when permanent solutions are unavailable. It is the antithesis of delay, in that it promotes progress instead of inaction. Responsible stewardship requires the use of mid-term remedies so that progress can be made in protecting human health and the environment now and in the future. It deals with waste in relatively short periods, say 20 years. After such a period, society can decide what to do with site cleanup for the next 20 years. However, the benefits of actions considered over the short term should not obscure the benefits of long-term solutions. If many 20-year periods are considered together, the costs of taking only the short-term view could be huge.

As mid-term remedies are put into place, it is important for DOE to continue developing permanent solutions to problems that resulted from past mistakes. In addition, responsible stewardship should promote waste-minimization and waste-reduction efforts to avoid repeating mistakes with newly generated waste.

References

Blush, Steven M. and Thomas H. Heitman. 1995 Train Wreck Along the River of Money: An Evaluation of the Hanford Cleanup, A Report for the U.S. Senate Committee on Energy and Natural Resources, Washington, D.C.

DOE (U.S. Department of Energy). 1995a. Closing the Circle on the Splitting of the Atom: The Environmental Legacy of Nuclear Weapons Production in the United States and What the Department of Energy is Doing About It. The U.S. Department of Energy, Office of Environmental Management, Office of Strategic Planning and Analysis (EM-4), Washington, D.C.

DOE (U.S. Department of Energy). 1995b. Estimating the Cold War Mortgage: The 1995 Baseline Environmental Management Report. Volume I, March 1995. U.S. Department of Energy, Office of Environmental Management, Washington, D.C.

GAO (U.S. General Accounting Office). 1994a. Federal Facilities: Agencies Slow to Define the Scope and Cost of Hazardous Waste Site Cleanups. Report to the Subcommittee on Investigations and Oversight, Committee on Public Works and Transportation, House of Representatives. GAO/RCED-94-73. April.

GAO (U.S. General Accounting Office). 1994b. Nuclear Cleanup: Completion of Standards and Effectiveness of Land Use Planning are Uncertain. Report to the Chairman, Committee on Governmental Affairs, U.S. Senate. GAO/RCED-94-144. August.

NRC (National Research Council). 1994. Ranking Hazardous-Waste Sites for Remedial Action. National Academy Press. Washington, D.C.

NRC (National Research Council). 1995. Technical Bases for Yucca Mountain Standards. National Academy Press. Washington, D.C.

OTA (U.S. Congress, Office of Technology Assessment). 1991. Complex Cleanup: The Environmental Legacy of Nuclear Weapons Production. OTA-O484. U.S. Government Printing Office, Washington, D.C.

49

Speaker's Task Force on Nuclear Cleanup and Tritium Production. 1995. Report to Speaker Newt Gingrich: "The Top 20 Ways to Turbocharge DOE Cleanup." Office of Congressman Richard Hastings, U.S. House of Representatives. August 4.

Appendix

VARIOUS PERSPECTIVES ON DOE'S ENVIRONMENTAL MANAGEMENT PROGRAM

This appendix was prepared by National Research Council staff to summarize relevant documents prepared by various organizations and individuals. The summaries focus on the regulatory aspects of the reports and are not intended to be comprehensive. The subcommittee has made no attempt to identify the reports with which it agrees or disagrees

Blueprint for Action and Cost Control at Hanford (May 3, 1995) summarizes the results of a meeting held on April 26–27, 1995, by the senior managers of DOE (headquarters and Richland), EPA (headquarters and Region 10), the Washington state Department of Ecology, and the major contractors (Westinghouse and Bechtel). The meeting addressed how to manage the cleanup of the Hanford site. Participants discussed ways to cut costs and increase the efficiency of regulatory measures. Five major kinds of action for the redirection of the Hanford cleanup were identified:

• Using a project-management approach that rewards action, promotes accountability, and controls costs. This could be accomplished by breaking up large projects into smaller discrete packages, tightening the chain of command, moving to performance-based incentives, and making project managers responsible for scope, safety, cost, and schedules.

• Reducing costs and increasing competition. Site contractors would use performance-based, fixed-price, and other incentives to control costs and maximize performance.

• Tracking and reporting cost savings. Independent reviews would be conducted to assess cost savings, and regulators would be involved in developing the scope of the task and in the assessment of the findings.

• Establishing target end points for cleanup and ensuring sitewide integration. This would involve using future land use as a tool for directing cleanup.

• Streamlining the regulatory process. The state of Washington and EPA committed to work together to divide the Hanford workload and to strive for a single regulator to make decisions on any given project. Regulators and DOE agreed to an early review of projects to ensure agreement on scope and direction. They will consider ways to avoid building costly new storage or disposal facilities and to defer construction of a waste-receiving and waste-processing facility. Regulators and DOE will jointly review regulations that apply to the management of mixed wastes. Regulators agreed to consider consolidation of documentation of overlapping regulation under a one-document approach. DOE, EPA, and the state agreed to launch a task force to examine specific regulations that apply to Hanford. DOE agreed to reduce its orders, both from headquarters and from Richland. There was agreement to consider acceptable reuse of facilities and reduce inventory of excess plant equipment and materials.

Train Wreck Along the River of Money—An Evaluation of the Hanford Cleanup was written at the request of the US Senate Committee on Energy and Natural Resources (Blush and Heitman, 1995) and focuses on the cleanup of the Hanford Nuclear Reservation in Washington state. The report presents criticisms that include the lack of regulatory balance (causing action without regard to cost or safety), compliance agreements that are more like partnerships, and lack of reasonable consideration of future land-use. The report recommends an evaluation of how DOE conducts cleanup activities, and it identifies several major changes in the overall regulatory process that are necessary to accomplish cleanup goals:

• Reform the legal and regulatory framework for cleanup.
• Resolve the question of the level of cleanup that will be required.
• Establish a negotiated level of funding based primarily on risk.
• Require DOE to undertake and maintain an integrated risk assessment as the primary basis for budgeting.
• Require DOE to produce and periodically update a long-range plan for cleanup that integrates all aspects of waste management, facility cleanup, and environmental restoration.

The US Office of Technology Assessment (OTA) report, *Complex Cleanup: The Environmental Legacy of Nuclear Weapons Production* (OTA, 1991) addresses the public-health effects of contamination, policy incentives, priority-setting, and risk and health assessment regarding DOE sites. The report faults the lack of regulatory standards that do not address past releases from the waste facilities and the contamination of soils and sediments both on site and off site. It also finds DOE's authority to enforce its own standards governing off-site radiation doses to present a serious problem.

OTA believes that the prospects for cleanup during the next several decades are relatively poor, and the report recommends the following policy incentives for improving DOE cleanup:

• Increase congressional oversight of restoration to improve performance.
• Increase public access to information.
• Strengthen site-monitoring programs.
• Improve the process for assessing potential health impacts of waste, evaluate the possibility of off-site health effects, and develop health-based priorities.
• Establish a new office to direct risk, health, and dose assessments.
• Establish a new program for off-site assessments.
• Establish an independent advisory board to guide exposure assessments and evaluations.
• Encourage more public and scientific participation in setting cleanup policy.
• Establish advisory boards with technical staff.
• Establish a national board to coordinate site-specific boards.
• Require DOE and others to consult with boards before key decisions.
• Provide outside regulation of DOE radioactive-waste management.
• Establish a national commission with regulatory and enforcement authority with respect to radioactive-waste management.

A statement given before the US Senate Committee on Energy and Natural Resources on March 22, 1995, contains Thomas Grumbly's vision for DOE's Environmental Management Program. He explained, in broad terms, that good progress has been made at the Hanford facility. He also gave a general outline of possible congressional action related to waste cleanup. The regulatory aspects of those suggestions were as follows:

• Establish realistic timelines for goals.
• Limit enforceable milestones to 3-year goals. Completion of goals requiring longer periods would not be enforceable.
• Allow for all penalties for noncompliance to be used to fund further risk reduction.

• Alter Superfund to codify land-use considerations and universal standards.
• Allow site-based budgeting and a 3-year budgeting cycle.

A state taskforce report, *Environmental Obligations at Federal Facilities and an Analysis of the Environmental Management Program of the Department of Energy* (June 2, 1995), finds many problems with the relationship between DOE and states. (Authors of the report include representatives of the states of Colorado, Washington, and Ohio.) It indicates that DOE has many regulatory failings that must be corrected, including lack of direction, insufficiency of contractor oversight, poor contracting mechanisms, and overreliance on weapons contractors with little environmental experience. The report finds that many regulations create overlaps between federal agencies and the states and that DOE is often rigid in its interpretation of regulations to the point where nothing is accomplished. The interested states can be more flexible and creative in their approach to waste cleanup than federal agencies. The report's suggested remedies include allowing qualified states to oversee DOE cleanup and clarifying the role of anticipated future landuse in priority-setting. Other proposed reforms are the following

• Provide for independent audits of DOE's environmental programs.
• Simplify and clarify regulations.
• Eliminate overlaps that create redundant oversight of cleanup.
• Allow states to exercise EPA's CERCLA authority or implement their own proven cleanup programs.
• Allow states to be sole regulators of cleanup at federal facilities.
• Clarify applicability of the Atomic Energy Act to waste management.
• Consider including enforceable deliverables in CERCLA agreements if all agree.
• Eliminate need for duplicate studies and reviews before cleanup.
• Clarify roles that anticipated future land uses play in remedy selection.

The report of the Environmental and Occupational/Public Health Standards Steering Group entitled *CERCLA Reauthorization: Opportunities for Improving Remedy Selection and Resource Allocation* (October 22, 1993) focuses on the improvement of CERCLA without completely rewriting the law by examining risk assessment, land-use planning, and ARARs. (Thirteen DOE laboratory directors chartered the steering group.) The group finds that the requirement of Superfund to comply with ARARs leads to excessive costs, which in turn discourages future landuse. The group sees the following as methods of improving site remediation

• Use local authorities and citizens in the early stages of risk assessment.
• Focus on risk reduction rather than residual risk.
• Use best estimates and probability distributions of critical data in risk assessment rather than the 95th percentile.

- Take realistic land-use assumptions and projections into account.
- Remove the "relevant and appropriate" section of the ARARs.

The General Accounting Office (GAO) report *Federal Facilities: Agencies Slow to Define the Scope and Cost of Hazardous Waste Site Cleanups* (GAO, 1994a) suggests the following amendments to CERCLA

- Require agencies to submit plans for cleanup to EPA.
- Require agencies to report annually to EPA on progress.
- Require agencies to develop and update cost estimates.
- Require EPA to report annually to Congress on agencies' progress.

The GAO report *Nuclear Cleanup: Completion of Standards and Effectiveness of Land Use Planning Are Uncertainties* (GAO, 1994b) focuses on the idea of land-use planning as related to radioactive-waste and hazardous-waste disposal and the problem of national standards for waste sites. It indicates that comprehensive cleanup standards are needed. In addition, EPA needs to provide more detailed 5-year reviews of sites with residual contamination.

A report to Speaker Newt Gingrich by the Speaker's Task Force on Nuclear Cleanup and Tritium Production (1995) provides *The Top 20 Ways to Turbocharge DOE Cleanup*

- Delegate regulatory authority over CERCLA to the states.
- Streamline or eliminate Superfund's ARARs.
- Consider final land and resource use before selecting remedies.
- Use risk assessment and cost-benefit analysis.
- Include various RCRA reforms in Superfund reauthorization.
- Amend RCRA's definition of allowable storage.
- Have RCRA consider reform of "mixture," "derived-from," and "contained-in" rules.
- Have RCRA consider reforming the Atomic Energy Act Exclusion.
- Integrate NEPA with other state and federal actions.
- Encourage a streamlined technology-permitting process.
- Streamline enforcement of health and safety regulations at sites.
- Grant broad decision-making authority to local DOE site managers.
- Streamline and localize the DOE order process.
- Reform federal indemnification procedures.
- Expedite opening of the Waste Isolation Pilot Project.
- Eliminate statutory metric-system requirements at sites.
- Leverage federal resources by allowing long-term privatization under incentive-based contracts.
- Ensure stable but flexible budgets for cleanup sites.
- Pass legislation to streamline the procurement process.
- Include the above provisions on a test or demonstration basis at one or more sites.

Part III
Priority-Setting, Timing, and Staging

SUBCOMMITTEE ON PRIORITY-SETTING, TIMING, AND STAGING

EDWIN H. CLARK II (*Chair*), President, Clean Sites, Inc.

HUGH J. CAMPBELL, Jr., Environmental Manager, DuPont

MARY R. ENGLISH, Associate Director, Energy, Environment, and Resources Center, University of Tennessee

DONALD R. GIBSON, Department Manager, Systems Analysis, TRW Environmental Safety Systems

ROBERT E. HAZEN, Chief, Bureau of Risk Assessment, New Jersey Department of Environmental Protection

THOMAS LESCHINE, Associate Professor, School of Marine Affairs, University of Washington

ROBERT H. NEILL, Director, Environmental Evaluation Group, New Mexico

LYNNE M. PRESLO, Senior Vice President, Technical Programs, Earth Tech

ANNE E. SMITH, Principal and Vice President, Decision Focus, Inc.

MERVYN L. TANO, General Counsel, Council of Energy Resource Tribes

Staff

Robert Andrews, Senior Program Officer
Patricia Jones, Project Assistant

Introduction

The Subcommittee on Priority-Setting, Timing, and Staging was established to review two areas of concern for Assistant Secretary Grumbly. The first, linked directly to priority-setting, dealt with

> the process of setting priorities for environmental management activities and how the process incorporates societal values, costs, current regulations, and risks to the environment, public health, and worker safety.

The second, focusing on the issues of timing and staging, dealt with

> how the environmental management program can schedule technology development and remediation and restoration efforts to maximize cost savings and minimize risks to the environment, public, and workers.

The two issues are closely related. When to undertake a particular activity and how best to organize its components —timing and staging—depend on the priority that the Department of Energy (DOE) attaches to completing the activity. Similarly, which activities should be undertaken first—priority—depends on the options, requirements, and advantages and disadvantages related to the timing and staging of the possible activities.

The subcommittee has concluded that priority-setting for DOE's Environmental Management Program has been problematic more for management reasons than for technical reasons. Important features that are essential for a sound priority-setting process at DOE, but that the subcommittee perceives as still lacking are the following:

• Clearly stated goals that are the fundamental end point of the priority-setting decisions.

• Stakeholder involvement in the priority-setting process that is both timely and integrated between local and national levels.

• Priority-setting that is comprehensive in scope (including intersite rankings among different geographic regions) and that goes beyond risk-ranking.

A range of organizational and cultural changes are also necessary to achieve as part of filling these gaps. Tools exist that can support most of the priority-setting needs in a technically sound manner once the management issues have been addressed, although they will need refining and adjustment to suit the specific needs. The rest of this report explains the management issues in more detail and provides some general guidance on the usefulness of different supporting tools.

Current Realities and Historical Context

The subcommittee recognizes the extreme difficulty of establishing priorities in an agency as complex as DOE. DOE has a number of missions. It has a national-defense mission, an energy-security mission, an environmental-quality mission, and a basic-research mission in support of its other missions. Moreover, DOE seeks to contribute to the nation's economic productivity by collaborating with industry wherever its established missions have provided an expertise that some industrial partner wishes to share. The programs of DOE that are undertaken in the pursuit of its missions inevitably have some goals that are inconsistent and some that are actually in conflict. In addition, DOE's priority-setting efforts will be affected by such factors as shrinking budgets; institutional relationships between DOE Headquarters, field offices, and contractors; and local and national political considerations. The subcommittee has sought to develop recommendations that will be useful and durable in the face of those disparate and changing circumstances.

DOE must and does decide what actions to take and how to spend its resources. In making its decisions and undertaking its actions, DOE is perforce establishing priorities. The subcommittee has gained, in the short time available, as much understanding as it could of the historical context and current practices for setting priorities in the DOE Office of Environmental Management (EM).

EM has its roots in a 1989 reorganization of DOE. At that time, it was apparent that the activities associated with waste management and environmental restoration were increasing in budget and complexity and that if the demands of federal and state regulators were to be met, a centralized planning process within DOE that could take into account the different situations across the entire DOE complex was needed. Before then, activities had been dictated largely by the desires of site managers, and their needs were not the principal concerns of the programmatic assistant secretaries who had responsibilities for the sites. With the creation of the Office for Environmental Restoration and Waste Management (later the Office of Environmental Management) came an attempt at more centralized planning; meanwhile DOE was continuing in its efforts to accommodate federal and state environment regulators who had only recently been given some jurisdiction over the sites.

While the 1989 reorganization was taking place, dramatic reductions occurred in the defense-related activities of DOE with the conclusion of several agreements between the former Soviet Union and the United States on reducing the number of nuclear weapons. DOE, states, and the Environmental Protection Agency (EPA) were establishing consent agreements establishing the outline of site-specific remediation efforts. It is not inconsequential that DOE has engaged in a massive environmental-remediation effort at the same time that the defense weapons complex has been declining. At some DOE sites, states and localities may see it as a high-priority matter of DOE's EM program to "fill the gap" with respect to employment and economic activity, whereas DOE and some taxpayers may see the expeditious, economic, and safe return of sites to the local communities as having high priority.

Another turn of events important for understanding the present context of the EM program was DOE's loss of some of its self-regulatory status in the environmental arena. Before 1980, DOE generally considered itself to be largely responsible for its own environmental performance. During the 1980's, however, state and federal environmental regulators gained partial jurisdiction over DOE sites—often in an atmosphere of distrust and hostility.

Today, many of the priorities in the EM program are set by the 100-odd compliance agreements that DOE has entered into with EPA and the states. These agreements have often become the primary "legal" drivers for EM budgetary decisions in DOE. Requests for funds from field sites and the later requests by DOE to the Congress for funding are driven largely by compliance with federal and state statutes and agreements.

EM developed and tested a highly sophisticated priority-setting tool for setting environmental restoration priorities called the Environmental Restoration Priority System (ERPS) from 1988 to 1991. However, the DOE discontinued the development and use of this system because of strong opposition by the states and other stakeholders who felt that the system had been developed without their input (Jenni et. al., 1995).

More recently EM established a set of 6 goals to guide its budget formulation process:

• Urgent risks and threats.

- Workplace safety.
- Managerial and financial control.
- Outcome orientation.
- Focused technology development.
- Strong partnerships with stakeholders.

The subcommittee defined its task as providing recommendations to DOE for improving its priority-setting system so that it allocates its available resources at its facilities to manage wastes, restore degraded environments, and otherwise protect the public's health and welfare in a cost-efficient and credible manner.

An Inclusive System

Priority-setting is often thought of in a limited sense, for instance, as applied to deciding which of many items on an agenda should be undertaken first or how much of an available budget should be spent. In the context of DOE, it can be used for screening activities, intra-site ranking of similar projects, intra-site ranking of projects in different areas, site-to-site ranking, etc.

To be successful, a priority-setting system[1] should be comprehensive in scope, addressing all forms of EM decisions and activities and addressing all DOE sites as a group. It must be technically sound, but it also needs to be rooted in the organization's basic visions about its purpose and goals. At the same time it is important to note that DOE does not require a sophisticated system to identify the highest-risk cases first; we recommend that DOE continue to act immediately to identify high-risk cases.

The subcommittee believes that priority-setting, timing, and staging are comprehensive planning activities that must take place within an organized and effective management context. Organization and management set the context for achieving progress in priority-setting, timing, and staging decisions. Progress in such decisions cannot be achieved simply through application of new or improved tools and analytical techniques. DOE requires a fundamental and pervasive change throughout the organization.

---

[1]The subcommittee uses the term "priority-setting system" as opposed to "priority-setting process" to emphasize that we believe that priority-setting must extend in many ways throughout many aspects of the DOE organization, and cannot be limited to a specific process that functions independently of these other parts of the system. The term "system" should *not* be taken to mean a specific tool or methodology.

This is not a trivial undertaking. Indeed, EM has a particularly daunting assemblage of sometimes inconsistent and even conflicting responsibilities and activities that it needs to harmonize if it is to establish an effective and efficient priority-setting system. EM must deal with:

• A need to balance fairness against efficiency and optimization.
• Substantial differences in what is perceived to be acceptable risk for workers, the general public, and the environment.
• Missions that range from the correction of environmental releases and the prevention of releases to safeguarding nuclear materials vital to the nations defense.
• A large variety and number of sites and contractors.
• Multiple regulatory requirements in DOE, EPA, Occupational Safety and Health Administration, state, and multiple-party agreements.
• Different beliefs of affected parties regarding the goal of ultimate land use.

All government organizations have to deal with such conflicts and justify their actions and requests for funds to fulfill their responsibilities. EM, however, faces a particularly great challenge because of its poor record of environmental restoration, the extremely high costs of carrying out its responsibilities (cost estimates for the cleanup alone exceed $230 billion dollars), and the absence of yardsticks to measure progress (DOE, 1995a).

EM recognizes its problems and has made initial attempts to improve the way in which it makes and implements decisions. The recent *Report to Congress, Risks and the Risk Debate: Searching for Common Ground* (DOE, 1995d), is a step toward recognizing that funding and other constraints will preclude complete environmental restoration and preservation to everyone's satisfaction. The subcommittee did not review the report and cannot endorse its specific methodology or accuracy. Although the report and the recently adopted changes in the DOE budget process demonstrate an initial effort to resolve the conflict between limited resources and unlimited wishes, future attempts at evaluating risks in relation to budget priorities should give more consideration to the optimum utilization of quantitative techniques and of outside peer-review panels, verify the values assigned to different elements of the risk assessment, and provide stakeholders with assurance of the quality of the analyses. It will also be important to include stakeholders earlier if the process is to serve as a means of consensus-building for setting priorities (NRC, 1994a). DOE has taken a step in this direction by initiating the Consortium for Risk Evaluation with Stakeholder Participation (CRESP) to provide independent peer review and structured interactions with stakeholders.

Although they constitute an improvement, the actions that the agency has already taken are only a start, and EM has not yet achieved a comprehensive and inclusive priority-setting system that will provide direction and guide the decisions that the agency must make in the coming years. Only when

DOE has established a more-comprehensive system will it be able to spend money wisely to manage risks to workers, the public, and the environment and to instill confidence in the public and Congress that it is doing so. Only by establishing a more-coherent system of priority-setting will DOE be able to break out of the incrementalism that characterizes its current decisions and prevents true priority-setting from taking place.

The agency needs to define what it is about in a coherent set of statements and processes that extend from the general and abstract to the specific and measurable, from defining its role to the specific steps that it will take to implement that role. It needs to define EM's mission, vision, goals, and objectives.

• *Mission.* Congress usually specifies an agency's mission in the legislation that defines its programs and activities. These are the work programs that allow the organization to achieve its vision. Are they consistent with the agency's vision? Are they consistent with one another? Do they define what the agency has to do to arrive at the state it has defined in its vision? How much flexibility does the agency have to modify these statements to make them consistent with its vision?

• *Vision.* The vision provides the agency, its staff, and the public an integrated look at the organization's future state. What does the agency want to accomplish? How does it want to view itself? How does it want the public to view it?

• *Goals.* Goals are targets for components within the mission, i.e., what the organization is trying to achieve in the short and long term. For example, is EM trying to maximize the amount of DOE land that will be available for public use? Is it trying to contain waste and contamination and restrict land use to the greatest possible extent to minimize costs? Is it going to have a comprehensive technology-development program to reduce costs of waste management and environmental restoration activities? EM must establish specific goals (both short-term and long-term) to implement a priority-setting system. After national goals have been established, sites should be allowed to develop alternatives in consultation with stakeholders and Headquarters. Sites, with strong input from local stakeholders, should relate each activity to national goals or their corresponding site-specific objectives. However, this should be done according to standard protocols, guidance, and formats developed by EM Headquarters to permit inter-site comparisons. Open reviews should be held at the local and national levels for site priority-setting. Revised priorities that result from stakeholder or EM review should be communicated to all parties.

• *Objectives.* Objectives are more-specific, short-term, and quantifiable measures of accomplishment in pursuit of the agency's goals, mission, and vision. Goals can pertain to many facilities or activities; objectives generally pertain to single facilities or activities. Objectives provide answers to such questions as these: What parts of each installation will be cleaned up with the intent of release to public use? What types of wastes will be accepted for storage or treatment at each installation? What will be the role of repositories as part of the long-range management of risks? What backup plans are made? Where will the repositories be, and what volumes of waste will they be able to accommodate? What areas of the current complex will retain long-term access restrictions? What types of risks will be managed through long-term DOE stewardship rather than complete remediation?

The success of a priority-setting system ultimately depends upon how well it is actually *implemented*. For example, will the vision for EM be achieved by dismantling all or selected DOE production facilities? Should EM establish regional waste repositories for ultimate disposal of certain wastes? Should EM target technology-development activities for the most-costly problems or problems with no current technical solution?

Attributes of a Priority-Setting System

An effective priority-setting system has several key attributes which must be manifest both in the system's development and in its implementation. Without them, systems can be developed but will have little impact and not last long. The attributes are important for priority-setting in any organization, but they are particularly important in systems intended to influence decisions in organizations that are as complex and subject to such diverse and changing pressures as EM. Although the subcommittee observed encouraging signs in some attributes—such as stakeholder involvement, work is needed in all of the following key attributes:

• *Permanence and consistency.* The subcommittee has observed a lack of consistency in EM's efforts to state its goals. Budget documents and other official pronouncements often began (rightly) with a statement of the organization's goals, but the statement commonly differed from those in other documents issued at the same time. Such deviations and inconsistency will substantially inhibit the effectiveness of a new priority-setting system. EM is attempting to modify substantially the operations of a large, complex organization that is known more for its inertia and rigidity than for its agility. To make such a change requires consistency in statements about where the organization should be headed. The subcommittee recommends that the priority-setting system be established through a careful process that involves substantial opportunity for input from the full range of stakeholders. The subcommittee also recommends that once established, the priority-setting system be described and implemented consistently.

• *Clarity and transparency.* The entire process, its development, exposition, and implementation, should be as clear and transparent to affected stakeholders as possible. Unfortunately, DOE has engendered a substantial legacy of suspicion and mistrust because of decades of operating secretly. It has made much progress already in reducing this mistrust. A clear, transparent priority-setting system will reinforce this trend and should encourage the early exchange of concerns to foster common conclusions.

• *Simplicity.* The simpler the priority-setting system and its tools are, the more likely it is to be followed and trusted. Although the associated methods should be scientifically defensible, they must also be understandable to affected parties. Because many of the criteria to be rated require subjective judgment and the inventories of toxic materials are incompletely defined, it is not always possible to establish scientific certainty. Hence, the system should not be so complex as to require elaborate analyses and consume an unreasonable amount of time to prepare, especially when the data to support great detail are not available. As more data become available or as the need for greater precision in estimating risks, costs, or benefits arises, then more complex analytical approaches are justified.

• *Stakeholder Involvement.* The legacy of low public trust in and credibility of DOE originated in the need for secrecy in some programs and authorities assigned by Congress for self-regulation. The Secretary has taken steps to involve people affected by DOE's actions in the decision-making process. This has been successful and should be continued formally. Stakeholders do not have authority to determine funding, but they should participate in and understand the basis of funding decisions. The inclusion of state and local stakeholders in this process for FY 1997 is laudable. DOE's experience, and the experience of other organizations in similar circumstances, suggest that regulators and public stakeholders need to participate to the greatest extent feasible in priority setting that leads to DOE budgetary decisions. (This point is similar to that made in the National Research Council's *Building Consensus* report (NRC, 1994a) with respect to DOE's use of risk assessment in its environmental remediation program.) However, public and stakeholder interest is strongly aligned with the interests of specific sites, and DOE's current mechanisms for public involvement appear to do a better job of promoting the budgetary stakes of particular sites than of facilitating intersite budgetary tradeoffs. Thus, while allowing for public participation, DOE must also fundamentally alter its budget-allocation process to allow for more-centralized setting of overall goals that promote the national interest. EM should apply the following principles related to stakeholder involvement:

—For stakeholder involvement in priority-setting to be knowing and intelligent DOE must provide stakeholders with all appropriate planning and budgeting guidance.

—Stakeholder involvement in priority-setting must occur at the installation level, the field-office level, and the Headquarters level. Therefore, DOE should tailor stakeholder involvement to specific priority-setting requirements, such as different types of stakeholder representatives and different types of stakeholder training.

—Stakeholder involvement in different EM program components—e.g., Community Leaders Network, the Military Toxics Project (a network of community groups concerned with environmental justice), Transportation External Coordinating Committee, Environmental Management Advisory Board, and State and Tribal Government Working Group (STGWG)—should be integrated into the overall priority-setting effort.

—Stakeholder involvement in priority-setting must be effective in helping EM to establish and resolve conflicts in field office and installation priorities and Headquarters priorities. Therefore, EM should annually evaluate stakeholder priority-setting efforts. The exercise should not be a one-time effort but should be an iterative process that encourages accountability of DOE field management and contractors.

Implementation of a Priority-Setting System

The most carefully conceived and well-thought-out priority-setting system will bring little improvement if it is not implemented coherently and comprehensively for all the activities that take place in the DOE EM Program.

It is often said that the primary function of priority-setting is to help an organization decide what it will **not** do. In the case of EM, for instance, three groupings of activities can be made as follows:

- Activities that provide a measurable benefit for the Program as defined on the basis of cost, risk management or risk reduction, and schedule.
- Activities that support a measurable benefit.
- Activities that do neither of those.

Activities in each of these groups are affected by different factors. The term used by EM is "driver." Those activities can be classified according to their drivers, specifically:

- *Required drivers* that necessitate a particular activity, such as triparty agreements, consent orders, and the Code of Federal Regulations.
- *Voluntary drivers* that support the activities of DOE's overall mission of increased efficiency, such as infrastructure needs and risk-reduction or risk-management needs.

Table 1 and Figure 1 depict the inter-relationships and overlaps of the three groups of EM activities and their drivers. The most basic goal of EM's priority-setting system should be to distinguish those activities that have or support measurable benefits from those that are extraneous and have no cost- or risk-reduction benefits. For example, activities that are either voluntarily or driven by regulation *and* provide a measurable benefit should be maintained and evaluated further to determine their exact priority, timing, and staging. Activities that neither provide nor promote or sustain measurable benefits *and yet* are voluntarily implemented should be eliminated. Those activities that are driven by regulation or law and that are identified as having no measurable benefits or do not support or sustain other beneficial activities, should be the subject of an effort by DOE to have those regulations modified or laws amended. Twenty-three state attorneys general have expressed a willingness to renegotiate previous commitments for environmental cleanups. DOE should aggressively explore these opportunities with the goal of reaching agreements that will result in faster and greater risk reduction, lower expenditures, and implementation plans that are more in accord with scientific and budgetary realities.

RELATIONSHIP OF OTHER MANAGEMENT SYSTEMS TO PRIORITY-SETTING

More must occur than the definition of mission, vision, goals, and objectives. DOE must also build an entire management structure in which the priority-setting system must function. This management system should include the following:

TABLE 1   EM Activities

	Measurable Benefit	Supports Measurable Benefit	Neither
Drivers Required by:			
DOE Order			
Other Regulation	X	X	seek changes
Compliance			
Agreement			
Law			
Voluntary Drivers	X	X	cease activity

NOTE: X = Evaluate risk, cost, and benefit for priority-setting, timing, and staging.

Activity Groupings

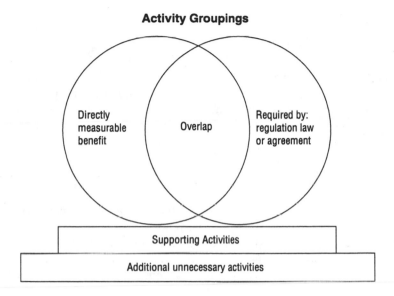

Utilization of an effective prioritization should result in:

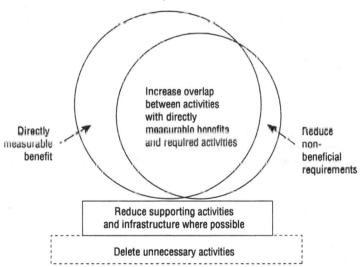

FIGURE 1　Activity Groupings

• Annual Budget formulation system.
• Personnel system.
• Contracting system.

Each of these systems will be discussed briefly. The key features which they must have to permit the effective implementation of the priority-setting system will then be described. There are three elements which should be common among all those systems: incentives, measures of performance, and feedback mechanisms to improve performance.

INCENTIVES, METRICS, AND FEEDBACK

There are a number of institutional barriers and disincentives to the effective setting of priorities that can be readily observed, and which several workshop participants noted. These barriers must be addressed. Doing so might require changes in how EM is organized and operates. Incentives will have to be created in a way that allows centralized goals to be achieved through decentralized decisions. Accountability, using accurate measures of performance, is key to aligning progress to DOE's vision. Particular examples of disincentives are as follows:

• *Lack of accountability for progress.* The current system appears to have no clear measures of progress and does not hold project or site managers accountable for achieving the progress desired. It is important to note that all too often progress is seen as meeting the nearest point in a schedule rather than moving toward an objective in an organized and rational way. All too often the pressures to meet the schedules are so important that consideration cannot be given to innovative technology, innovative approaches to the process, or any other change that might be desirable in the big picture.

• *Self-perpetuation as a goal.* Self-perpetuation seems to be a strong, if unexpressed, goal driving the system. Progress in cleaning up is often in conflict with this goal and often appears to lose in the conflict.

• *Costs as a "good," risks as an "asset."* Because the funding allocated to a site is often influenced by the magnitude of the risks at the site and the estimated cost of cleaning up its contamination, there is a strong incentive to overestimate both risks and costs to increase the amount of money available and the salaries, responsibility, attention, and employment that typically result from large budgets.

As already noted by DOE, fundamental values of the organization might have to be altered, and a new culture might have to be instilled so that the changed values are spread throughout the organization. For example, increasing budgets might be valued now as a sign of success, but would be antithetical to an EM program in which success were defined as continuously improving the productivity of the program. At DOE facilities, contractors and workers have a strong incentive to make work take as long as possible; it guarantees them a job, eliminates relocation problems, and so on. DOE needs to develop incentives that will strongly counter that inherent inertia. If, for instance, it wants to reduce its workforce and complete the cleanup job early, it might provide large bonuses and relocation allowances to workers who achieve those goals. It should also be noted that such changes might extend to the participating public as well and might require an adjustment of expectations regarding the public's inclusion in the DOE decision-making process.

Effective implementation of a priority-setting system and its companion management systems requires constant evaluation of how well the systems help to accomplish the vision, mission, goals, and objectives on which it is based. Without a way to evaluate that, managers will be unable to evaluate the effectiveness of the department's operations and make corrections when they begin to diverge from their goals.

Thus, it is essential that DOE's managers and contractors be required to measure what was accomplished for the funds spent and to quantify future improvements for the funds requested. The general perception in recent years has been that public funds for environmental restoration have not been well spent, but there are no concrete measures of progress to substantiate this perception. The number of facilities decontaminated or removed from a status where monitoring is necessary and the relative cost per square foot of building space are better measures than the number of reports filed with a regulatory agency. Hence, progress must be measured in such terms as reduction in a radionuclide or chemical concentration in an aquifer or the effect of preventing a release of an aerosol or effluent from a source, not in the traditional government terms of, e.g., the frequency of inspections or the number of hours of stakeholder consultation.

A very useful metric is periodic ''benchmarking'' comparison with the best of the private-sector efforts. EM should calculate the cost of common environmental-management efforts undertaken by the department and compare them with those for equivalent activities in the private sector. Examples include low-level waste disposal at Chem-Nuclear in South Carolina, Envirocare in Utah, and U.S. Ecology in Washington; mixed-waste management subject to RCRA; and use of soil covers to minimize leachate problems. Such comparisons will indicate whether spending is out of line with the private sector.

Other mechanisms might include

- A national stakeholders review panel to review results of analyses.
- Technical evaluation of the validity of the analyses by a contractor.
- Red-team or inspector general evaluations.

The final step required for a successful management system, including a priority-setting system, is a feedback mechanism that allows corrections in the system when it is deviating from the vision, mission, goals and objectives that the department has established. The effectiveness of this feedback system will depend substantially upon the accuracy and relevance of the metrics incorporated in it.

BUDGETING

In the budget process the role of Headquarters is to set general policy guidance and secure funding through Congress. The sites have the specific knowledge of those activities with the highest potential for harm, those that can be delayed in implementing remedial action, and those with the best potential for risk reduction. EM management at Headquarters understands the overall budget constraints placed on the Program. The product of the interaction between the sites and Headquarters—the budget request—should reflect their mutual understanding and the input of stakeholders.

EM's primary mechanism for implementing priority-setting across its entire program is its internal budgeting process. The priority-setting system and the budget system are interconnected, since projects and programs must be prioritized for funding. For FY 1997, under a directive of Assistant Secretary Grumbly, the program justifications of specific projects and programs were developed with reference to four priorities:

• Protection of worker and public health and safety and the environment.
• Safety, security, and stabilization of special nuclear materials.
• Compliance with federal, state, and local regulations and statutes, related enforceable compliance and cleanup agreements, and DOE orders.
• Compliance with other agreements to which DOE is a signatory (memorandum, Asst. Secretary Grumbly to Distribution, Feb. 13, 1995).

In addition, high priority was given to those investments which significantly drive down future costs as well as those that stabilize nuclear materials and facilities. This is a departure from earlier DOE priorities. At the outset of the EM Program the extent of the remediation task and its total costs were poorly understood. DOE was under attack on all fronts as being insufficiently aware of and responsive to its environmental problems. Reducing future costs was lower in priority than immediate regulatory compliance. These priorities have changed, and this change has contributed to the difficulties experienced by DOE employees and contractors.

As we understand it, FY 1997 development of the budget proceeded as follows:

• National (DOE Headquarters) direction was provided to each of DOE's site offices and apparently was focused on funding targets.
• Sites set priorities for their work and submitted them to DOE Headquarters.

- After discussions between the sites and management, the sites modified some priorities.
- A national meeting was held (involving all DOE sites and Headquarters) at which Mr. Grumbly made decisions regarding the site and Headquarters priorities.
- Those decisions were later shared with stakeholders, and stakeholder questions regarding both the process and the resulting priorities were answered.
- A "lessons learned" meeting was held to discuss the process and make appropriate changes.

These last three steps are unique to the DOE EM Program and special permission was given by the Office of Management and Budget for this new process of including stakeholders in the budget formulation process. Further modifications, intended to make the process more transparent to stakeholders, are being developed by EM for FY 1998.

One problem that the subcommittee noted in the resulting 1997 budget-formulation process is inappropriate "bundling." All priority-setting schemes rely to some extent on the assumption that the objects being compared are roughly similar. "Bundling" is the process of lumping dissimilar things into packages that are then thought of as constituting a single activity. In the case of DOE's Environmental Remediation Program, bundles of proposed remedial actions might be made up of elements that if examined individually, would be seen to pose different types of risks or to require different kinds of processing from an engineering and technical standpoint. Such bundling can erode the ability of priority-setting systems to make useful distinctions, inasmuch as the benefits of reducing the risks associated with high-risk components are offset in risk-benefit comparisons by the added costs of taking care of costly but lower-risk elements in the same package.

A variety of forces, ranging from the internal dynamics of DOE's budgeting process to DOE compliance agreements with states and federal regulators, appear to be creating this bundling problem. A prominent example of such bundling occurred in the Tank Waste Remediation System (TWRS) at Hanford. Originally, in the Hanford site's 1987 environmental-impact statement, the contents of the single- and double-shell tanks at the site were assigned to different disposition sequences. The contents of the double-shell tanks were to be retrieved, treated, and disposed of, but action on the single-shell tank contents was to be deferred (DOE, 1991). In the 1989 *Tri-Party Agreement* with the state of Washington and EPA, however, all tanks were bundled into the common retrieval, treatment, and disposal path that became TWRS. The planned TWRS retrieval and processing sequence gave rise to a single "high public safety" risk data sheet in the recent DOE document *Risks and the Risk Debate: Searching for Common Ground* (DOE, 1995b), June 1995, Appendix C, with a projected 5-year cost of nearly $400 million. Even though most double-shell tanks at Hanford probably pose much lower risk to the public than do leaking single-shell tanks and tanks on Hanford's "watch" list, all are treated in the same way, and all costs are counted against high-priority risk reduction in DOE's *Common Ground* document.

DOE should address such bundling problems by re-examining how disparate projects and program elements are grouped for budgeting purposes with an eye to regrouping those that pose similar risks. The subcommittee believes that that could be done by a central audit (either by Headquarters or by an external independent party) that sets a target of examining perhaps 10% of the activities listed on the risk data sheets per year. An alternative might be to set a threshold on projected cost and examine all activities above the threshold. If inappropriate bundles are identified, they should be disaggregated and reranked. DOE should also establish some process for rewarding units that bundle activities properly and penalizing units that do not. The result of such an audit, however conducted, would increase the number of activities in the budgeting process in such a way that the costs associated with individual activities would, on the average, be lower—in some cases, the subcommittee believes, by a considerable amount.

The Appendix includes one approach to budgetary priority-setting that meets these requirements and satisfies the attributes listed in the previous section.

*

PERSONNEL

Budgeting is only one of the elements of management that drive how the DOE operates. The personnel system is another, and it might have an even greater impact on how effectively EM implements its priority-setting system.

Government personnel systems are notoriously unresponsive, and the DOE system is notorious among government systems. Such an unresponsive system can substantially inhibit the implementation of needed changes. Staff both at Headquarters and in the field should be encouraged to develop innovative approaches to solve problems, rewarded if successful, and not penalized if unsuccessful. If the personnel system is not changed to reflect or incorporate these changes, the implementation of new priorities will be much more difficult and, unless substantial pressure is continuously applied, is likely to revert gradually back to its former shape with its former priorities.

Another subcommittee has addressed the problems associated with the current personnel system in greater detail and has made some recommendations regarding how it could be made more responsive. If that is not done and if the personnel system is not made to conform to the new priority-setting system, the implementation of the priority-setting requirements is likely to be seriously retarded.

CONTRACTING

Much of the work undertaken under the DOE's auspices is done by contractors, not employees. It is perhaps even more important to modify the contracting system than it is to modify the personnel system. The former contracting system, established primarily on a "cost-plus" basis, rewarded input rather than output, effort rather than accomplishment. The subcommittee recognizes that EM has begun to make some important changes in its contracting system—most notably in the Rocky Flats performance-based contracts that were recently awarded. Those are important changes, and we applaud them.

Another subcommittee has dealt in more detail with the contracting system. We point out that basing contracts only on performance rather than on effort and providing rewards to contractors for achievement are crucial to the success of the changes that EM is attempting to implement in priority-setting. To do so properly, however, requires the completion of the process of defining a vision, missions, goals, and objectives described above. Only then can the department be sure that the performance measures incorporated in the contracts accurately reflect and incorporate the goals of the department.

Criteria for Setting Priorities

Perhaps the most important step in establishing an effective priority-setting system is identifying, defining, and selecting priority-setting criteria. It is rarely an easy task, particularly in an organization as complex and with as many divergent goals as EM. The subcommittee recommends that the DOE undertake the identification, definition, and selection carefully and deliberately, with substantial input from all the stakeholders who have to accept the final process if it is to succeed.

The first step should be to identify the full list of factors that should be taken into account in setting priorities. We suggest that the DOE consider developing and utilizing the full list of factors through a "bottom-up" approach. That is, stakeholders at the individual facilities would be asked to review an initial list of criteria developed by EM and recommend modifications or additions to it. A good starting place for developing this list would be the extensive list of evaluation criteria developed for and incorporated into the ERPS model (see Figure 2). The reviews and suggestions would be aggregated through the field offices and combined at Headquarters. A process of consolidation and redefinition would follow. The goal of this process would be to derive a manageable set of priority factors that are inclusive and clearly defined so that they are interpreted consistently by everyone involved in the EM priority-setting system, from Headquarters staff to local advisory panels and other stakeholders.

To ensure that the process is comprehensive and the criteria clear, the DOE might want to consider involving any of the following groups in the winnowing and defining:

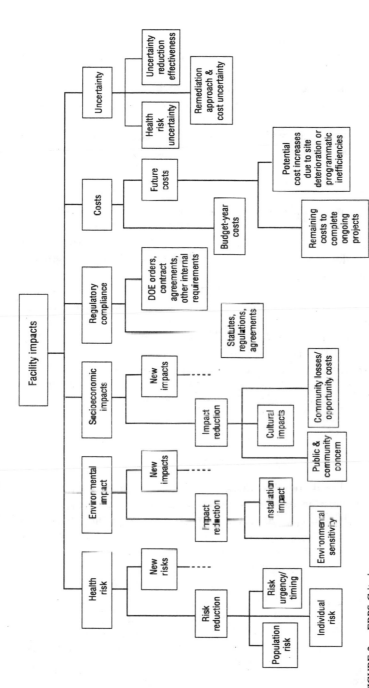

FIGURE 2   ERPS Criteria

SOURCE: Lee Merkhofer, Applied Decision Analysis, Inc. Presentation at the National Academy of Sciences, June 27, 1995.

NOTE: Dashed lines below "New risks" and "New impacts" indicate subobjective structures similar to those under "Risk reduction" or impact seduction," respectively.

• A national stakeholders panel.
• Focus groups, which can identify issues that need to be considered in the priority-setting system.
• Site-specific stakeholder advisory groups, which can help to ensure that site-specific considerations are duly integrated into a more centralized system of priority-setting.
• Technical review panels, which can assess the adequacy of information being generated and help to identify analytic or information gaps and shortcomings.

Although it is important to identify and define the full set of relevant criteria, the actual process of establishing priorities is likely to be driven by only one to three of them, and the department must get agreement on which, from the full list, are the most-important priority-setting factors. That should be done at the Headquarters level with the full involvement of the Assistant Secretary and Secretary.

The primary factors should demonstrate two characteristics: they can be quantified on a scale that allows activities to be ranked from most important to least important, and the factor metric, i.e., the means of estimating the extent to which each activity satisfies these factors, is determined consistently for all the activities. The value placed on the primary-factor metrics must be independent of where an activity would occur and free of any rater biases.

Two criteria that are now treated as primary factors and that would probably retain this pre-eminence in any priority-setting system are risk and regulatory considerations.

USING RISK

Some measure of risk or risk reduction associated with an activity is likely to be and should be a primary factor. Examples of possible primary factors related to risk are the risks that would exist were the activity not undertaken, the reduction in risk that would result from undertaking the activity, and the risk reduction per dollar of expenditure that would be associated with undertaking the activity.

The subcommittee recommends that, to the extent possible, a single set of general methodological guidelines for risk assessment be applied to all sites and proposed activities. We recognize that establishing such a set of guidelines may be difficult. Currently, there is no consistent methodology for assessing risks at DOE sites (NRC, 1994a). Unfortunately, some of these inconsistencies are imposed on the DOE by different regulatory agencies demanding different degrees of rigor in risk assessments (NRC, 1994a). However, without some consistency in conducting risk assessments, it will be very difficult to set priorities coherently.

Risk assessment methodology need not depend upon sophisticated quantitative models and analytical techniques. Indeed, it is appropriate that the degree of complexity of risk assessments varies from site to site depending on the amount of data available and the purpose for which the risk assessment is being done. The view that a risk assessment process is absolutely essential for dealing effectively with the risks at DOE facilities must be tempered by the need to draw from existing data, which sometimes cannot support an exhaustive risk assessment (NRC, 1994a). In the early stages of priority-setting, a simpler, less quantitative risk assessment may be sufficient for managers to make preliminary decisions as to whether further assessment is necessary. The subcommittee believes that using these screening-level (possibly judgmental or qualitative) risk assessments is possible. As appropriate (i.e., where it is essential for the decision-maker and where sufficient data exist), more quantitative analyses should be utilized. EM should not be deterred from making priority-setting decisions where there are limitations in data and knowledge. These limitations should be noted explicitly as EM pursues its obligation to make decisions. A note of caution in the use of screening-level risk assessments: because they are often quite conservative and may overstate risk, their use is most appropriate for decisions about whether there is no any potential for significant risk or whether more analysis is needed.

Future land-use assumptions can have a profound effect on the estimation of risk. Sites that will be occupied in the future pose many more exposure opportunities than sites that will be left uninhabited. Local stakeholders must have a significant voice in decisions about future land-use. However, EM must ensure that these decisions are reasonable and that the exposure assumptions associated with the selected land-uses assumptions are consistent across sites and facilities sharing the same future land-use scenario. One might also wish to present the range in the risks by assuming perpetual isolation and unrestricted residential use, in addition to each site's selected land-use scenario.

Socioeconomic factors affecting stakeholder groups and Indian tribes may also be important to incorporate in risk assessments. A key to the successful identification and treatment of these factors is the early involvement of the interested parties in these efforts (NRC, 1994a).

Tools

In this section, we describe the range of types of priority-setting tools that might be considered for adoption as part of a re-engineered DOE and EM budget allocation process. This is kept brief, and is intended only to highlight the range of acceptable approaches that may be useful. An earlier NRC committee report, *Ranking Hazardous Waste Sites For Remedial Action* (NRC, 1994b) provides a synopsis of the qualities of good tools, and reviews of three specific existing tools that could be of relevance here. Rather than repeat such discussion, a section of that report describing the characteristics of a good priority-setting tool is reproduced as an appendix to this subcommittee's report.

Use of any tools in a priority-setting system should have the same attributes identified earlier in this report as desirable for the entire system, such as providing substantial opportunity for input from stakeholders on their values and concerns and input from technical experts on complex technical issues. Priority-setting tools generate alternatives for action and evaluate alternatives and combinations of alternatives against clearly articulated, consciously weighted decision criteria.

The main concern in selecting a tool is that the content be aligned with and supportive of an institution's goals. Choosing the right tool to support a priority-setting system involves some balancing. Tools that are attractive on process grounds might not necessarily lead to good outcomes. Formal, mathematical tools that are easy to use and understand might fail to embody sound decision logic or, in their reliance on subjective judgments, lead to results that are unstable in the face of small changes in the circumstances under which they are applied. The DOE needs to consider these and other process-related characteristics as it develops or selects tools to support its priority-setting system.

In all cases, it is important to emphasize that the output of decision-aiding tools should not be the end points of the priority-setting system. Once specific options or strategies have been identified, analyzed, and assessed, decisions must still be made by accountable decision-makers regarding which options to take, and appropriate institutional and procedural enabling actions must still be taken.

The subcommittee is of the opinion that many tools that meet the DOE's needs for effective priority-setting are already available. As emphasized above, the greater barriers to more effective priority-setting are in creating an organization that allows difficult decisions to be confronted and tradeoffs to be made. Once those organizational issues have been addressed, existing priority-setting tools and approaches should provide many useful options consistent with the types of decisions that need to be made. We do not feel that trying to develop new tools would add significant value. Any system-development efforts should be targeted to improving the credibility and usefulness of tools already available in the field, either by addressing specific technical issues that have been identified in the tools or by tailoring existing systems to the goals of the DOE-EM process.

There is an important distinction to keep in mind between tools that support site-ranking and tools that support actual priority-setting. Site-ranking can place a number of risky situations in an order of risk, but such ranking does not indicate how to allocate dollars to a range of possible cleanup activities. Priority-setting, by contrast, may involve consideration of many other criteria, such as costs and incremental risk reduction. Site-ranking considering only risk can be useful for setting priorities for site assessment but not be efficient or effective for setting priorities for cleanup activities themselves. Site-ranking tools can range from strictly qualitative check-list approaches, through such scoring systems as EPA's Hazard Ranking System (HRS), to quantitative risk-assessment tools.

True priority-setting techniques, in contrast, provide enough information to assess whether to take action and what types of action to take. They are able to assist in identifying reasonable tradeoffs across sites and across activities. Thus, priority-setting tools require:

• Activity-specific information.
• Incremental information (e.g., how much change in risk is associated with an action).
• Explicit recognition of the multiple goals that an institution is trying to address.

A priority-setting system can be qualitative or quantitative. One concern with the usual quantitative approaches is that they are "black boxes" and that the fundamental nature of differences among alternatives is lost when all the decision criteria are collapsed into a single numeraire, such as utils or dollars. (Thus, they are weak in transparency and to some extent in the clarity with which facts are distinguished from values from the observer's perspective.) It is not necessary, however, to address the multicriteria tradeoffs required in priority-setting through strictly quantitative techniques, such as Multi-Attribute Utility Analysis (MAU). All that is required of a priority-setting tool is that it explicitly recognize the nature of tradeoffs inherent in specific choices of actions. Alternative multicriteria approaches that avoid focusing on a single score or value estimate might also be useful.

The drawback of such approaches is that information about multiple criteria can be voluminous and difficult for decision-makers to assimilate if not summarized into comparable (unimetric) units. It is possible, however, to devise visual displays in a variety of formats that assist interested parties and decision-makers in mentally processing and understanding the tradeoffs embodied in multicriteria information. Such approaches avoid the step of having the system produce specific rankings, or "recommended" actions; they leave such conclusions to be drawn by each person viewing the results, but they provide the basis for justifying one's own conclusions.

In addition to greater transparency, nonaggregating multicriteria approaches have the advantage of using neither a single person's preferences nor a highly uncertain representation of societal preferences, so they avoid potential concerns with bias. Nonaggregating approaches also allow exploration of alternative viewpoints in a format that is more conducive to consensus-building: the process helps people to visualize the perspective that other interested parties have with respect to a particular choice.[2]

At the site and facility levels, a number of formal priority-setting tools appear to be in use for setting budget and other priorities. One example is the Laboratory Integration and Prioritization System (LIPS), which is a multiattribute utility-based approach that was developed at Los Alamos National Laboratory and used in demonstration applications at a number of DOE sites (B. Anderson at the subcommittee's workshop of June 26–27, 1995). The subcommittee did not review LIPS and cannot provide an overall evaluation, but we believe that LIPS should be carefully considered for its alignment with DOE's goals, once DOE's overall priority-setting system is more effectively structured. LIPS might not be readily applied to the *intersite*

---

[2]An example of such an approach is EPA's multicriteria decision-support system developed for setting priorities among strategies for adapting to global climate change, called the Adaptation Strategy Evaluator. EPA's experience in initial applications of this approach is that it is particularly useful for identifying strategic directions without the detailed analysis required of CBA, for gaining insight into why some strategies appear to meet goals better than others, and for building consensus.

priority-setting step, but it can readily be used for priority-setting among the many activities possible at a given location. An intersite priority-setting tool could then be applied with such site inputs as LIPS might be able to produce.

ERPS is a detailed application of the MAU approach that is tailored explicitly to deal with the many unique features of DOE's EM organization in the process of allocating budgets *among sites*. Although questions have been raised on particular technical points, its main limitations are that it had poor stakeholder involvement during its development and depends excessively on judgments made by the model builders rather than reflecting widespread stakeholder consensus; it is perhaps too ambitious in attempting to incorporate all values, no matter how subjective and qualitative, into a single quantitative metric; and, as a result it failed to meet the objectives of clarity, transparency, and simplicity.

This subcommittee has not reviewed ERPS in detail and so cannot make any comprehensive evaluation of it. Nevertheless, it stands as a major contribution toward an MAU-based priority-setting tool. It is unlikely that any other MAU-based tool would substantially improve on the foundations that exist in ERPS, and we recommend that the DOE allocate tool-development resources to improving the usefulness of ERPS rather than trying to develop a new MAU model to replace it. Improvement of a system that has already been heavily funded is generally more appropriate than starting from the beginning on a new system.

It must be recognized that the budget-allocation process that DOE faces is extremely complex, and MAU-type analyses, which combine all ranking criteria according to a system of weights, will probably be essential for obtaining a systemwide sense of priorities. However, DOE might wish to consider using techniques that keep individual priority-setting factors separate in conjunction with those that merge priority-setting factors. In this way DOE can focus on generic priority-setting issues, such as technology development versus immediate cleanup, and also provide better communication and interaction with interested parties as DOE goes through its priority-setting system.

Conclusions

Establishing a robust priority-setting system for an organization as diverse and complex as EM is clearly not a simple task. The subcommittee has focused more on the attributes and characteristics of an effective priority-setting system than on the specific tools or criteria that it might employ. The organizational environment in which such a system is established and implemented may well be as important as the system itself. This organizational environment will probably be more important than the specific tools or criteria the system employs, and it will also help to determine whether the system satisfies the attributes of permanency, consistency, clarity, transparency, simplicity, and stakeholder involvement that the subcommittee recommends.

An effective priority-setting system is more than just a process of making budget decisions. It needs to incorporate specific goals and objectives so that progress can be measured. It needs to include metrics for measuring how much progress is truly being made towards accomplishing these goals and objectives. It needs to incorporate feedback mechanisms that will stimulate corrections in the decision-making process if the metrics demonstrate inadequate progress. It needs to be reflected in all of the personnel, contracting, and other administrative and decision-making processes in EM, not just in the budget process. It must be accompanied by a clear series of incentives and disincentives that reflect goals and reinforce the system. It needs to demonstrate that decisions in all these areas, both within DOE sites and across sites, are being made consistently.

Again, establishing such a system is not a simple task. It will require substantial effort and input by Headquarters and site personnel, technical experts, regulators at the state and federal level, elected officials, the general public, and other stakeholders. The subcommittee believes, however, that this is an investment that should be made. The decisions EM is making will affect the allocation of tens of billions of dollars, determine how significant human health and environmental risks are addressed, affect the jobs of hundreds of thousands of workers, determine the future use of millions of acres of land, affect local and regional economies throughout the nation, and have an impact on national and international security. Clearly, these are decisions that need to be made carefully and correctly. Clearly, the investment is worth it.

The subcommittee does not want to suggest that all decision-making be put on hold until this investment is completed. Decisions must be and will be made regardless of whether an adequate priority-setting system exists. Certainly the DOE has some potentially high-risk situations that it must address. It does not require a sophisticated system to address these worst cases first, and we recommend that it do so. We also recommend that, in the interim, EM postpone those actions that do not significantly reduce risks or save money, and that are not required by current laws. Even when there appear to be current legal requirements, if the action is not addressing a significant risk, we recommend that the agency "push back" on the regulatory drivers. Ultimately, in this period of tight federal budgets, everyone will benefit if the agency can demonstrate that it is efficiently spending its resources on the most serious problems.

In short, there is plenty to do and there is a need to do it right. We believe that EM has taken some useful first steps, but it has many more to go.

References

DOE (U.S. Department of Energy). 1991. Tank Waste Disposal Program Redefinition. Prepared for the US DOE Office of Environmental Restoration and Waste Management. WHC-EP-0475. Rev.0. Washington, D.C.

DOE (U.S. Department of Energy). 1995a. Estimating the Cold War Mortgage: The 1995 Baseline Environmental Management Report. Volume I, March 1995. U.S. Department of Energy, Office of Environmental Management, Washington, D.C.

DOE (U.S. Department of Energy). 1995b. Risks and the Risk Debate: Searching for Common Ground "The First Step". The U.S. Department of Energy, Office of Environmental Management, Washington, D.C.

Jenni, Karen E., Miley W. Merkhofer and Carol Williams. *The Rise of a Risk-Based Priority System: Lessons from DOE's Environmental Restoration Priority System.* Accepted for publication by *Risk Analysis.* April 10, 1995.

NRC (National Research Council). 1994a. Building Consensus Through Risk Assessment and Risk Management in the Department of Energy's Environmental Remediation Program. National Research Council, Washington, D.C.

NRC (National Research Council). 1994b. Ranking Hazardous-Waste Sites for Remedial Action. National Academy Press. Washington, D.C.

Appendix
ONE APPROACH

During the subcommittee's deliberations, one member was tasked with developing an approach to priority-setting that would incorporate the various characteristics and attributes that the subcommittee believed were important. This appendix contains the result of that effort.

The proposal stimulated some controversy. Some subcommittee members thought it was a useful contribution which would clearly improve the budget formulation and other priority setting processes. Other members and reviewers considered it naive, academic, infeasible, and bureaucratic. Because of time constraints, the subcommittee was unable to perfect the proposal in response to these comments.

Thus the original proposal is included in this appendix, without the subcommittee's modification or endorsement, in the belief that it may contain some concepts that would be of interest and value to the Department.

The proposed framework builds upon the existing budgeting process and incorporates substantial involvement at the local level although leaving the decision-making ultimately at the national level. The framework begins with the clear articulation of DOE's priorities for EM expenditures and, proceeding through a nine-step process, finally gives some leeway to the local stakeholders to make a final choice about the priorities which best suit them.

Define Priorities: The proposed process would begin with EM, with substantial input from its various stakeholders, identifying the full list of factors that should be taken into account in setting priorities.

We suggest that DOE consider developing the full list of factors through a "bottom-up" approach. In such a process, the stakeholders at the individual facilities would be asked to review an initial list of factors and recommend modifications or additions to it.

These reviews and suggestions would be aggregated through the regional offices and combined at Headquarters. They would then undergo a process of consolidation and redefinition.

The goal of this process would be to come up with a manageable set of priority factors which are inclusive and clearly defined so that they are interpreted consistently by everyone involved in the EM priority-setting system, from Headquarters staff to local advisory panels and other stakeholders. DOE might want to consider involving a national stakeholders panel in this winnowing and definition process to ensure that the criteria of inclusiveness and clarity are met.

Select Primary Factor: The second step would be for DOE to select from among this list what it considers to be the most important priority-setting factor. This should be done at the Headquarters level with the full involvement of the Assistant Secretary and Secretary.

The primary factor would most likely be related to the risk associated with an activity. Examples of possible primary factors related to risk would be the risk that would exist were the activity undertaken, the reduction in risk that would result from undertaking the activity, or the risk reduction per dollar spent that would be associated with undertaking the activity.

It is important that the primary factor demonstrate two characteristics. One is that it can be quantified on a scale that allows activities to be ranked from most important to least important. The second is that the factor metric, i.e., the means of estimating the extent to which each activity satisfies this factor, be determined consistently across all of the activities. The value placed on the primary factor metric must be independent of where the activity would occur and free of any biases that the rater might have. Assuming that risk or risk reduction is a component of the primary factor, this second criterion suggests the advantage of having risk assessments carried out by a neutral third party.

Appoint Trustees for Other Factors: The third step would be to designate trustees to represent each of the other priority-setting factors. These trustees should be Headquarters employees, probably assigned to the budget office. Their responsibility would be to help EM achieve the best possible priority-setting result by ensuring that the issue for which they are the trustee is given adequate consideration in this process.

Their primary loyalty must be to the DOE, not to the issue. Their goal should be to ensure that EM's budget and other priority-setting systems reflect rational, efficient, and equitable weighing of all of the DOE's priorities. Their responsibility would be to see that their factor is given due consideration.

This does not mean maximum consideration. They should not operate as representatives of particular interests who try to maximize the resources dedicated to these interests. They should operate as trustees of these interests who ensure that the interests are given fair and adequate consideration.

This is a subtle but important distinction. It is to clarify their role as trustees rather than representatives that argue for them being employed in the Headquarters budget office. Another mechanism for discouraging them from taking on a representational rather then a trustee role would be to periodically reassign factors among the trustees.

To fulfill their responsibility they should learn as much as possible about why local stakeholders may have ranked various activities as very important according to their factor. In many cases this importance would be communicated to them by the stakeholders most concerned about this factor. If this communication does not occur naturally, the trustee would have a responsibility to obtain such information by talking to the local interests after reviewing the activity summary sheets described below.

Activity Summary Sheets: The budgeting or other priority-setting system should be based upon activity summary sheets similar to those DOE is apparently using at present. The summary sheets should include a terse description of the activity and a rating of the importance of the activity with respect to each of the priority-setting factors. To the extent possible, the rating for the primary factor should be quantitative on a cardinal scale. The ratings for the other factors would also benefit from reasonable quantification, but a qualitative indication of relative importance would suffice as well.

The development of these summary sheets should begin at the local level and be fully informed by review and contributions of local advisory panels and other stakeholder input. There may be a need to modify the ratings as the summary sheets are reviewed at the regional and national level in order to improve their commensurability, but the reasons for such modifications should be indicated and be part of the public record.

These summary sheets would provide the basis for, and a public record of, the priority-setting system.

Initial Ranking: The activities would be initially ranked, from most important to least important, according to the primary factor. If the evaluation of this factor across activities has met the criteria of objectivity and consistency, this initial ranking would be a straightforward tabulation of the information on the summary sheets.

The results of this initial ranking would then be distributed to the trustees and possibly throughout the system including the local stakeholder groups, in preparation of the re-ranking process.

Re-Ranking: During the re-ranking process the trustees would argue for activities to be raised or lowered in the ranking because of the importance of the factor for which they are the trustee.

For example, the trustee representing cultural values might argue for a particular activity to be raised in the ranking because of the extent to which this activity would satisfy a strong tribal, cultural, or spiritual value in spite of the activity's relatively low impact on human health risks.

The trustee representing the cost reduction priority might argue that certain activities be lowered in the ranking because they address risks that would be attenuated naturally if nothing were done. A containment and wait strategy might result in significant cost savings in such a case over the long run.

The trustee representing compliance requirements, on the other hand, might argue that the same activity be raised in the ranking because it is explicitly identified in a tri-party agreement, and failing to undertake this activity could result in a strong enforcement action by the applicable regulatory agency.

The trustee representing EM's innovative technology priority might argue that a particular innovative technology activity be raised in the ranking and several clean up activities be lowered, because the innovative technology activity promises to achieve significant cost savings in these types of cleanups in the future. If such a re-ranking were agreed upon, the individuals responsible for those cleanup activities would have an incentive to ensure that the technology development activity achieved that goal.

To the extent possible, re-ranking decisions would be made by a consensus of the trustees and the individual responsible for presenting the ranking to the Assistant Secretary (usually the budget director). Where consensus is not reached, the disagreement would be noted for final resolution by the Assistant Secretary.

In order to satisfy the objective of transparency, the reasons for any re-ranking decisions should be made explicit, written down on the activity summary sheet, and made part of the public record of the priority-setting exercise.

Proposed Final Ranking: The proposed final ranking would be presented to the Assistant Secretary along with a summary of the disputes that could not be resolved by the re-ranking committee. If there were an unreasonably large number of unresolved disputes, each of the trustees might be limited to identifying one or two disputes that the particular trustee wanted raised to the Assistant Secretary's level. The ranking would not be changed for those disputes that were not raised.

If a large number of disputes resulted from disagreement among the trustees about the relative importance that should be accorded particular priority factors, this question should be raised to the Assistant Secretary for guidance before the re-ranking is completed. The goal would be to have only the most important issues raised to the Assistant Secretary's level.

Final Ranking: The Assistant Secretary would make decisions regarding the disputes raised to his or her level to create EM's final ranking.

Depending upon the priority-setting system that is being undertaken, EM's final ranking will usually undergo further reviews and modifications before it becomes truly final. Depending upon the rules that the DOE, the Office of Management and Budget, or others might have imposed upon this process, it may not be possible to make the final EM ranking or subsequent modifications public.

Nevertheless, at some point there will be a final "ranking" of some sort which will be public. In the case of the budget, the form of this final ranking will be a list of those activities which are included in the budget. The more public this process is, the more it will satisfy the criteria of transparency and credibility that are important for a priority-setting system.

A Possible Final Local Review: The process described has substantial local involvement in defining and rating the importance of the activities. However, the ranking and re-ranking are carried out, albeit informed by this local information and assessment, predominately at the national level.

The DOE may, if it is allowed to do so, want to provide the local level with a final opportunity to modify the ranking. This could be done by allowing the local site-specific advisory group to propose the substitution of a local activity that is below the cutoff line (e.g., unfunded in the budget) for another local activity of equivalent cost that is above the cutoff line. The presumption would be that such a substitution would be allowed as long as it was not unreasonably inconsistent with national priorities, particularly the primary priority factor.

Part IV
Utilization of Science, Engineering, and Technology

SUBCOMMITTEE ON UTILIZATION OF SCIENCE, ENGINEERING, AND TECHNOLOGY

FRANK L. PARKER (*Chair*), Distinguished Professor of Environmental and Water Resources Engineering, Vanderbilt University
JOHN F. AHEARNE, Lecturer in Public Policy, Duke University
CHARLES B. ANDREWS, Vice President, S.S. Papadopulos & Associates, Inc.
EDGAR BERKEY, President, National Environmental Technology Applications Center, University of Pittsburgh Applied Research Center
HAROLD K. FORSEN, Senior Vice President (retired), Bechtel Hanford, Inc.
WALTER W. KOVALICK, Director, Technology Innovation Office, Office of Solid Waste and Emergency Response, U.S. Environmental Protection Agency
MICHAEL L. MASTRACCI, Director, Innovative Technology Programs, TECHMATICS, Inc.
PHILIP A. PALMER, Senior Consultant, DuPont Specialty Chemicals, E.I. du Pont de Nemours & Company
REBECCA T. PARKIN, Director of Scientific, Professional, and Section Affairs, American Public Health Administration
ALFRED SCHNEIDER, Professor of Nuclear Engineering (retired), Georgia Institute of Technology
CHRISTINE A. SHOEMAKER, Professor, School of Civil and Environmental Engineering, Cornell University
C. HERB WARD, Foyt Family Chair of Engineering and Director, Energy and Environmental Systems Institute, Rice University
JOHN T. WHETTEN, Senior Applications Consultant, Motorola
RAYMOND G. WYMER, Consultant, Chemical Technology Division, Oak Ridge National Laboratory

Staff

Stephen Parker, Associate Executive Director
Karyanil Thomas, Senior Program Officer
Anita Hall, Administrative Assistant

Introduction

This is the report of the Subcommittee on the Utilization of Science, Engineering, and Technology. Biographical information on the members is provided in Appendix B. This subcommittee examined how the Office of Environmental Management's (EM) technology-development efforts could best utilize science, engineering, and knowledge of the health consequences of contaminated Department of Energy sites.

The subcommittee met on July 11 14, 1995. In a workshop format, the subcommittee heard presentations from representatives of Department headquarters, Department sites, contractors at Department sites, Environmental Protection Agency (EPA) headquarters, citizen groups, environmental advocacy groups, and industries engaged in large environmental remediation efforts. The workshop agenda and list of participants are included in Appendixes B and D, respectively.

A roundtable discussion was held after the formal presentations to explore some of the relevant issues. The participants identified what they considered to be the most important matters that need to be addressed, and the subcommittee used the results of the roundtable discussion and contents of the presentations, as well as the experience of the participants, to develop a framework for this report.

ENVIRONMENTAL PROBLEMS FACING
THE DEPARTMENT OF ENERGY

US involvement in the nuclear arms race for 50 years resulted in the development of a vast research, production, and testing network that has come to be known as the nuclear weapons complex. Over $300 billion (in 1995 dollars) has been invested in the activities of this complex. Today, the Department is faced with the largest environmental remediation task in the federal government. Remediation will entail radiation hazards, vast volumes of contaminated water and soil, and over 7,000 contaminated structures (DOE, 1995a). DOE must characterize, treat, and dispose of hazardous and radioactive wastes that have been accumulating for some 50 years at 120 sites in 36 states and territories. Over the last 5 years, the Department has spent more than $25 billion in identifying, characterizing, and managing its waste and in assessing the nature of the remediation necessary for its sites and facilities. The Department estimates that remediation could cost a total of $200–350 billion and take 75 years to complete (DOE, 1995b). This does not include the cost of cleaning most contaminated ground waters or currently active facilities.

EM is also responsible for conducting waste minimization and pollution prevention for all of the Department of Energy. The variety and volume of the Department's activities make that effort a challenge in its own right. The Department has nearly 30 laboratories that employ about 50,000 people who are engaged in the full spectrum of scientific and engineering disciplines. Moreover, the Department is engaged in the largest weapons-dismantlement effort in its history. Those activities and current remediation efforts are subject to an effort announced by Secretary O'Leary to reduce the amount of toxic waste that the Department's facilities produce by 50% by 1999 (DOE, 1995c).

PROBLEMS IN CORRECTING THE LEGACY

EM was established in 1989 to deal with the environmental legacy of the nuclear arms race. The EM Program has six goals:

- To eliminate and manage urgent risks in the system.
- To emphasize health and safety for workers and the public.
- To establish a system that is managerially and financially in control.
- To demonstrate tangible results.
- To focus technology development on identifying and overcoming obstacles to progress.
- To establish a stronger partnership between the Department and its stakeholders.

The Department's historical culture of secrecy and its contamination problems at nuclear weapons sites have profoundly affected public attitudes and opinions. Citizens have expressed concern at the community and national levels about both the potential health and environmental impacts of conditions within the DOE complex, urging that sites be cleaned up. Technology to characterize and remediate contaminated soil or water or to treat, store, and dispose of accumulated waste safely is not necessarily available. Waste-disposal standards and cleanup goals for the environment have not been developed, agreed to, or applied at each site (EPA, 1995; OTA, 1991).

Technology development is one element of the EM Program. It includes research and development of new environmental technologies whose use is intended to make Department operations and remediation "better, faster, cheaper, safer, and in compliance with existing regulatory requirements" (DOE, 1995c). EM has estimated that technology development could save 10–22% in costs of remediation, treatment, and disposal, depending on the amount of cleanup performed (DOE, 1995b), and EM's Office of Technology Development estimates a savings of at least $10 billion. For fiscal year 1995, technology development accounted for 6.5% of the Department's EM budget (waste management and treatment and facility stabilization and decommissioning accounted for 66.0%, and environmental restoration accounted for 27.5%).

Findings and Recommendations

This section provides a summary of the findings and recommendations that the subcommittee came to during its deliberations. The first subsection contains general observations about the Environmental Management Program and sets the context for the specifics regarding the use of science, engineering, and technology in the program.

GENERAL GUIDANCE

• We recommend a life-cycle approach in which environmental consideration is given to all processes and products, with a goal of eliminating or drastically reducing waste streams at every stage of the activity. This should apply to both mission activities of the Department and all elements of the Department's environmental remediation efforts, which consist essentially of site characterization, remediation, waste management, and waste disposal. Implementation will require the creation of incentives and the removal of disincentives. For example, programmatic groups within the Department should use their own operational funds to pay EM for the management and disposal of the wastes that they generate, rather than use the current system whereby EM provides the service and the funding. That would provide a definite incentive for programmatic groups to minimize waste and to use appropriate technology.

• Goals specific enough to be used for decision-making (which incorporates such tools as risk-based and cost-benefit analysis) should be established for remediation. The goals should be developed with stakeholder input. They should provide clear end points for risk-based cleanup for various land-use options, levels of long-term maintenance and monitoring, and schedules for accomplishing tasks based on difficulty. These goals should be set first at the national level with a clearly identified process that can be used to develop site-specific goals that will be within the limits of the national goals.

• Without knowledge of proposed land use and cleanup levels, the identification and implementation of appropriate technology for remediation is not possible. The emphasis that the Department has placed on these goals for future land-use plans and cleanup levels with stakeholder input is commendable. Although there is more to be done in this regard, failure to resolve these points completely should not be a barrier to continuing remediation activity. A possible way to overcome this barrier until these land-use and cleanup level goals are established is to use existing models, such as the Multimedia Environmental Pollutants Assessment System (MEPAS) and Argonne National Laboratory's RESRAD, to estimate the risks associated with the present system, the technology that will reduce the risks, and the cost to reach a socially acceptable solution.

• Planning and technology development must be iterative to take into account changing conditions and new developments in the light of the expectation that the remediation process will continue for at least 75 years and that needs and funding will change. That expectation should not be interpreted as a mandate for inaction.

• EM has vastly improved the working relationship between its site managers and stakeholders in the surrounding communities. It could make further progress by establishing incentives for Department officials and communities to make planning decisions that would result in more cost-effective and timely actions.

• Site actions must be consistent with state and federal laws; with compliance agreements among the Department of Energy, Environmental Protection Agency, and the states; with the wishes of citizen advisory groups; and with resource limitations. Guidelines and limitations can be in conflict with each other or be unrealistic. The system has become overconstrained. To achieve consistency, the Department should attempt, as industry does, to take advantage of flexibility in laws and compliance agreements. However, industry does not have as many constraints as the Department (e.g., in the form of site-specific advisory boards and compliance agreements), and for the Department, relief might require legislation.

• The Department should manage its contractors by focusing on seeing that the outcomes desired are reached (i.e., performance goals). It should not manage the day-to-day activities performed by contractors in reaching those goals.

• The Department has taken preliminary steps in the creation of a Department-wide uniform process to evaluate risks to the environment and to health with the publication of *Risks and the Risk Debate: Searching for Common Ground* (DOE, 1995d). The subcommittee did not review the report and cannot endorse its specific methodology or accuracy. Ultimately, the process should be able to identify the locations and situations across all DOE sites that pose the most serious imminent risks to the public, to workers at Department sites, and to the environment. Imminent risks to the environment and to public and worker health should have the highest priority for action. For nonimminent risks, risk assessment should be used to identify the benefits of risk reduction as part of overall cost-benefit analyses, which should form the basis for further priority-setting and for the timely resolution of contamination problems that must be addressed as required by law or compliance agreements.

TECHNOLOGY SELECTION AND DEVELOPMENT

• An explicit, comprehensive approach is needed to identify technology needs, select candidate technologies, and pursue their development. A key to the success of this process is that it be intimately linked with identified customer needs (i.e., site-specific application) and that it use quantitative tools, such as risk assessment and cost-benefit analysis. The process of technology selection must be iterative so that technologies under development reflect recent advances. The Department has made substantial efforts toward establishing such a comprehensive approach by the establishment of its focus areas for technology development. We support the further refinement of this framework and its decision-making processes. The Department should be vigilant in ensuring programwide and facilitywide implementation of this approach.

• The Department must dramatically improve its research and technology development outreach. That can be accomplished only by opening the Department's research and development program to all qualified individuals and organizations regardless of type or location. Concomitantly with the opening of the EM R&D procurement system, a broad-based system of external peer review must be carefully implemented and monitored to ensure that the best proposals are selected.

• Technology selection should incorporate a knowledgeable independent review group that has no vested interests in the outcome and that includes people from outside the Department who work in the commercial use of technologies.

• At the time of selection and throughout technology development, care should be taken that the products of technology development can be modified for similar applications throughout the Department complex. To the extent that technologies under development have the potential for use at a level that could support commercial development, the Department should become an early partner of commercial companies to encourage the development of the technologies by the private sector.

• Incentives should be provided for the development of technologies that reduce waste generation, that lower costs of remediation, or that improve safety.

• The Department must link technology development to technology demonstration and utilization programs. At all stages of the process, efforts should be made to inform potential users of the existence and performance of newly developed technology.

• The technology-development process proposed by the Department includes multiple points of analysis and evaluation (gates) where further development must be justified. Analysis should include quantitative tools, such as risk analysis and cost-benefit analysis (to degrees of detail that depend on the stage of technology development).[3] Such analyses must be benchmarked against available technologies, technologies under development in the Department, and technologies available in the broader commercial sector.

• There has not been a strong relationship between technology development and basic research. Technology development (already strongly influenced by technology users) must be strongly coupled to research and development at both the basic and the applied levels. The Department has recently begun efforts to improve this relationship (between the Office of Energy Research and Environmental Management) and it should continue to make this relationship a strong interactive one whereby technology-development needs can influence how basic-research budgets are allocated and vice versa. As in the case of technology development, basic research should be performed by the most appropriate institution as determined by competitive peer review.

• The decision as to whether National Laboratories, universities, or industry should take the lead in the development of any particular technology should be based on a competitive process that undergoes external review, not by formula or some other form of entitlement. Often, forming teams or partners among the different groups for the development of a particular technology is the most effective approach.

• National Laboratories constitute an extraordinary technical resource both in capability and in size. It must be recognized, however, that the Laboratories are unique in culture and expertise (especially in the case of nuclear materials); this can be both an advantage and a disadvantage in bringing new technologies to bear in restoration activities. There must be strong external benchmarking

---

[3]In cost-benefit analysis, costs should include both life-cycle costs and short-term costs. Life-cycle cost is an estimate of the full cost of implementing a technology over its expected life according to a discounted present-value analysis that uses various interest rates (including 0%). Benefits can include some of the following: decreasing risk of contamination for a population, increasing reliability of the method to contain pollution or to remediate, decreasing production of secondary waste, increasing safety of workers in the EM Program, and developing methods that might have wide use or commercial value.

and peer review within National Laboratories. The Laboratories must be open to procurement of outside capabilities even when the main body of the R&D fits within the Laboratories.

• As with all participants in technology development, the Laboratories should structure their efforts to be responsive to the technology customers.

• Many of the Department's waste-management issues are not peculiar to the Department—they are issues that are faced by private industries and by the Department of Defense as well. The Department should use fully the expertise and talent available in universities, industry, and other federal agencies. The role of industry and universities should have several elements: as sources of peer review, as collaborators in technology development, and as primary participants in technology development.

TECHNOLOGY UTILIZATION

• During testing and demonstration on a federal facility, the Department should indemnify a technology developer against an unplanned contamination of the environment, but not against failure to properly perform the work. Site operators and the local stakeholders who have taken risks in deciding to utilize innovative technology should be rewarded, not penalized, if a technology fails.

• All procurement approaches for developed technology must include provisions for testing and validation of technologies in the context of constraints of actual problems. The possibility of some degree of failure to meet target criteria or goals of well-conceived projects must be accommodated without excessive penalties.

• A group of competent, trained and experienced scientists, engineers, technicians, and support personnel must be maintained at Department sites to be able to judge the viability and facilitate the introduction of innovative technologies. It is essential in ensuring the successful introduction and utilization of technologies.

• In most cases, the site operating contractor must retain the responsibility of final approval for the use of proposed technology to the extent that it must ensure the health and safety of people both on the site and in the community around the sites and ensure preservation of the investment in the site.

Policy

The subcommittee believes that several issues must be addressed by DOE if it is to use scientific and engineering information successfully in its EM Program. It must have a vision of how it wishes to go about its mission activities. It must have clear and specific goals by which to accomplish its mission and do so in a way that fulfills its vision. There needs to be a clear decision-making process to support the establishment of goals and their implementation. This section discusses these topics.

THE VISION

US industry is refocusing and substantially broadening its vision of environmental management. The Department of Energy should do likewise. For current products and processes, that means setting pollution-prevention goals and acknowledging that the most effective way to reach them is to incorporate environmental criteria into experimental, process, and product designs.

The subcommittee recommends a life-cycle approach to ensure that environmental consideration is given to all processes and products, with a goal of eliminating or drastically reducing waste streams at every stage of the activity. In other words, the Department should pay more attention to the "front end" of the production cycle to minimize or eliminate what comes out the "back end." Generally, it is much more effective from both environmental and cost standpoints to eliminate waste at the source (source reduction) than to try to reduce the volume or toxicity of waste once it is generated.

That approach is appropriate for both programmatic activities (e.g., materials-development research) and remedial activities (e.g., preparation of high-level waste in storage tanks for eventual disposal).

Implementing this strategy will require incentives and removal of disincentives. Programs and operational groups should be expected to pay for the waste they generate. The current budget for EM provides funds for waste disposal for both the various ongoing programmatic activities of the Department and remedial-action programs. When a materials-development research program has to make a decision about what process to use in the laboratory, it does not have to give consideration to the costs of disposal of different alternative waste streams, because the EM Program has programmatic and budget responsibility for waste disposal. The research program in this example has no incentive to internalize the costs of disposal. If the research program had to provide funds to EM for the services rendered for waste disposal, incentives for waste minimization by the researchers would be in place. Additionally, waste minimization and pollution prevention should be evaluation criteria in performance review. Programs and groups should be rewarded for reducing and eliminating waste. Funding requests should be biased in favor of projects that have a strong life-cycle waste-minimization and pollution-prevention component and toward researchers who have demonstrated relevant concerns. It might be useful to develop public-recognition schemes for successful researchers.

Environmental remediation and decommissioning should not affect health or the environment adversely. Consideration of the life-cycle environmental cost of different remediation options should be included in cost-benefit decisions.

GOALS

The president of Clean Sites, Edwin H. Clark, succinctly described the problem facing many within the EM Program, including Department employees, contractors, and local citizens: "If you don't have hard statements of goals, it is difficult to figure out what to do to achieve them."

The Department and EM have produced many statements of goals, such as that in the latest risk report: "The primary focus of the [EM] program is to reduce the health and safety risks from radioactive and hazardous waste and contamination . . ." (DOE, 1995d). These were valuable when first promulgated, to lay out the philosophy of the new administration. However, when they continue to be the primary goals, they become pious statements that cannot be used to make decisions at Department sites and facilities.

The Department should take the steps necessary to establish goals with sufficient specificity for decision-making. The goals should be set first at the national level with a clearly identified process that can be used to develop site-specific goals. They should incorporate land-use planning and enable risk-based and cost-based decision-making.

In the absence of clear and accepted goals, it should not be surprising that decisions are postponed or constantly revisited, that "the remediation program has accomplished far less than many wish" (DOE, 1995e), and that the Department "has been severely criticized because of the small amount of visible cleanup that has been accomplished" (DOE, 1995e).

One important example of a goal that needs greater specificity is just what level of cleanup is acceptable. "How clean is clean enough?" is not a new issue. It has been a prominent question at least since the passage of the National Environmental Protection Act (NEPA) in 1970. The question cannot be answered in the abstract or general sense. It is a site-specific decision incorporating many of the variables previously discussed. That few sites have determined those levels is a measure of the difficulty in doing so. However, as the Department remediation program reaches a funding level of many billions of dollars per year and the Department estimates that the program will last three-fourths of a century, this seemingly intractable issue must be addressed. Reasonable bounds of a range of such levels should be determined nationally.

We recognize that effective goals cannot be established simply by executive pronouncement. It requires involvement of the interested and affected parties. At the national level, EM could turn to the Environmental Management Advisory Board (EMAB) to recommend such goals; EMAB is composed of a broad range of people—technical experts, representatives of state governments, and local stakeholders. It might also be appropriate for the Department to propose establishing national goals by legislation, after development by the various stakeholders.

Another approach that might be tried is often used in industry when major changes are seen to be required. A small group of employees from different levels of the organization, including middle-level managers, are sent off for 6–12 months, relieved of all other responsibilities, and given the task of coming up with a solution to the major problem. A similar approach was used by the Environmental Protection Agency in its writing of *Unfinished Business*, in what became a fundamental study of EPA's allocation of efforts, to identify the disparity between what the agency's experts believed were the greatest risks and where EPA was focusing its resources, primarily in response to Congressional direction.

Without knowledge of land-use goals and cleanup-level goals, the identification of needed technology is difficult. There are ways to analyze situations that can help those making decisions about what technology to apply or develop, even when the goals are not final. The first report of the NRC Committee on Environmental Management Technology stated: "Evaluation of technological alternatives and optimization should consider the systematic use of comparative risk and risk/benefit assessment'' (NRC, 1995). We recognize that EM recently, in response to a Congressional request, produced a first step in evaluating the risks associated with the many activities and facilities in the EM complex (*Risks and the Risk Debate: Searching for Common Ground "The First Step"* (DOE, 1995d)). However, this is, as its title suggests, only a first step. EM should continue to develop a risk-based approach by having risk assessment done of the major activities under the EM umbrella. Risk assessment is especially useful when priorities must be set and decisions about human (worker and public) health and environmental health must be balanced against costs. The process should be open, so that the results will be understood by both the Department and stakeholders. It should undergo peer review by outside panels.

Risk assessments, which take several iterations to approach useful results, should compare the risks at the several major sites to enable prudent allocations of resources and to decide their sequence (NRC, 1994). Ultimately, the process should be capable of identifying the locations and situations that pose the most serious risks across the nation to the public, to workers at Department sites, and to the environment. Imminent risks should have the highest priority for action. For nonimminent risks, risk assessment should be used to identify the benefits of risk reduction as part of overall cost-benefit analyses, which should form the basis for further priority-setting and for the timely resolution of contamination problems that must be addressed as required by law or compliance agreements.

A serious obstacle to remediation of sites is that the major factors that contribute to high costs in the remediation program have not been identified. Without that information, it is impossible to structure a cost-effective technology-development program. But the identification of needed technology is not possible without land-use goals and cleanup-level goals. Risk assessment can provide a way to overcome this barrier. Such existing models as MEPAS and RESRAD can be used to determine the risks associated with the proposed process or technology and compare it to a base case, that is, the technology most likely to be used today without further development. The use of those models in the past has been sparse because too few data were available. In some cases, the calculations may be too poorly supported because the input data are not sufficient and the models may not fit well. An effort to combine existing cost and risk numbers for activities may nevertheless be useful, in connection with dialogue with stakeholders on priorities for site remediation. However, the cost and residual risk for this base case could be determined with data from the BEMR (DOE, 1995b) and *Risks and the Risk Debate: Searching for Common Ground* (DOE, 1995d) reports. From this base case, the factors contributing the most to costs could be identified with reasonable probability. Once identified, the ''cost drivers'' could be analyzed with the models mentioned above to estimate what cost and risk changes would result from changes in land-use goals, cleanup-level goals, and technology used. Standard decision theory can be used to see what is gained in risk reduction for each incremental increase in the cost of cleanup. The outcome of the process might well be a radical restructuring of goals, priorities, what is remediated, to what degree, and at what time. To be successful, such a process must be open, transparent, and inclusive from the very beginning. Stakeholders must be able to see the costs and risks associated with different options for the operation of Department facilities in their communities and for the remediation of different sites. In a number of situations where this information has been provided, stakeholders have supported decisions that would surprise critics of substantive stakeholder participation (for example, the far reaching land-use decisions at the Hanford, Washington and Fernald, Ohio sites that resulted from the deliberations of the Hanford Site Use Working Group and the Fernald Citizens Task Force, respectively).

At the local level, goals that are consistent with the national-level goals, but that take local factors into consideration, should be established. It might not be possible to establish national-level goals first, but it could be possible to reach local agreement. We recommend that EM continue to work with site contractors and stakeholders to establish waste-management and cleanup goals that are realistic, i.e., recognize health risks, resource constraints, and the state of technology. The approach being developed by several states to develop and test models for interstate cooperation on testing, evaluation, and permitting of innovative technologies, such as that under the auspices of the Western Governors Association (WGA), might accomplish some of those aims.

It should be recognized that the analytical approach to goal-setting for land use and cleanup levels described above is the basis for an iterative procedure or a comparative analysis that should be used to set priorities for technology development and to elucidate the effects of different land-use goals and cleanup-level goals. Exact values are not needed; the values need only be ranked. In an iterative process, a perfect analysis is not necessary at each stage. The important thing is to proceed, and that means not investing too much time and money in the process at the early stages.

The fact that the remediation process is going to continue for over 75 years, at a minimum, affects the approach to technology selection and development. Rushing to remediate now, instead of appropriately characterizing a site or developing a "better" technology, might be the most expensive approach to an already-expensive problem. Planning and technology development must be iterative because conditions will change and new developments will take place.

Moreover, there need not be the fixation to get it right the first time as the mix of remedies will change over time as the results of the remediation research become available. At that point the Records of Decision required by regulatory agencies and agreed to earlier on specific activities for remediation can also be changed (just as they are now being changed regularly).

Even in the absence of national goals for cleanup or land use, EM must function in many regulatory systems. Site actions must be consistent with state and federal laws; with compliance agreements among the Department of Energy, Environmental Protection Agency, and the states; with the wishes of citizen advisory groups; and with resource limitations. Such guidelines and limitations can be in conflict with each other or be unrealistic. The system has become overconstrained. The Department should attempt, as industry does, to take advantage of existing flexibility in laws and compliance agreements aggressively. However, industry does not have as many constraints as the Department; according to the report *Train Wreck Along the River of Money* (Blush and Heitman, 1995), the wishes of citizen advisory boards and compliance agreements among the Department, EPA, and states have resulted in this overconstrained situation. Pat Whitfield, a former senior Department of Energy official, stated at this subcommittee's workshop that the "agreements were totally unrealistic on the day they were signed." Agreements should be changed, frank discussion must be held with site advisory groups, and legislation might be required.

Finally, goals should be set within a framework that provides incentives for agency officials and communities to make decisions. One suggestion was proposed in recent Congressional testimony on Superfund reauthorization: "Communities might be more willing to accept lower cost remediation if a portion of the savings would accrue to the local communities for such things as infrastructure development, improved schools, etc." (Parker, 1995).

PROCESS

EM has completed useful efforts to implement a new approach to its decision-making processes for technology selection, development, and utilization (DOE, 1994), but the subcommittee noted that decisions are made on differing bases or in some cases even by default. As EM has acknowledged, an explicit, comprehensive approach is needed to identify technology-development needs, opportunities, and applications. As this process evolves, EM should consider the following points of emphasis:

• The types, scale, and scope of problems to be addressed should be clearly defined.
• The type of decision-making process to be used should be based on the performance outcomes desired. That will clarify whether the process needs to be iterative—moving from a screening level of analysis to a more-detailed (possibly more-quantitative and data-based) approach—and whether it should use relative or absolute standards of judgment.

• The essential elements or tools to be used in the process should be stated and defined. For example, risk assessment and cost-benefit analysis might be valuable in summarizing and synthesizing scientific, economic, and public-policy information.

• Specific criteria should be developed for each element of each step in the decision-making process.

• Input from focus-area staff, project-technology leads, external experts, and stakeholders might be needed at different points in the process.

• Peer review should be used in the decision-making process. The peer-review system should exclude those who might be considered to have a conflict of interest. The peer-review groups should include members from outside the Department. Members of external peer-review groups who later develop conflicts of interest should be quickly removed from peer status. A peer-review system with the highest standards would go far in changing the insular image of the Department held by many and the common impression that review of an extramural R&D proposal by Department staff constitutes peer review.

• Feedback should be obtained from technology decision-makers and users on the results of the process to ensure routine evaluation and timely improvement of decision-making processes.

• Incentives should be provided to ensure timely closure in decision-making processes.

Technology Selection and Development

CUSTOMER NEEDS

The selection of technologies for development beyond basic and applied research activities is a key step in the overall technology-development process of the Department. If technology selection is done properly, the selected technologies should be able to move through the complete development process and lead to solutions of identified problems. If it is done poorly, it can result in wasted resources, in customer dissatisfaction, and in lingering problems.

At its most fundamental level, successful technology development is a product of meeting customer needs by solving their problems to an acceptable degree. Where technology development takes place independently of customer (and stakeholder) needs, the rate of technology deployment is low. Where the needs of potential customers (and stakeholders) are identified and considered from the beginning of the development process, the likelihood of eventual technology acceptance and use is high.

The subcommittee recommends that the Department's technology-selection process be intimately linked with identified customer needs. We believe that the most important step that EM can take in this regard is to ensure that a structured process is implemented and consistently applied to require consideration of customer needs explicitly and seriously from the beginning of the process.

FOCUS AREAS

The EM technology-development program designated five priorities or "focus areas" for technology development:

- Mixed-waste characterization, treatment, and disposal.
- Radioactive tank-waste remediation.
- Contaminant plume, containment, and remediation.
- Landfill stabilization.
- Facility transitioning, decommission, and final disposition.

The purpose of the focused approach is to bring together users and developers to decrease cost, decrease risk, and do what "cannot be done." In addition to the focus areas, the Department has identified several cross-cutting or common areas: characterization, monitoring, and sensors; efficient separations and processing; robotics; and technology transfer.

The subcommittee thinks that the focus areas that have been defined provide an appropriate structure for accomplishing this objective. The focus areas provide a forum for bringing together technology developers, technology users, potential industrial partners, and other stakeholders for the purpose of developing technical products that can meet customer requirements. We endorse and validate this approach as being closer to a market-driven or user-driven system than any technology-development procedure previously used by the Department.

However, we are concerned that implementation of the focus areas has fallen short of the intended mark primarily because user and customer requirements have not yet been fully integrated into the decision-making process for selecting new technologies. Some members of the subcommittee have observed a general indifference to the process on the part of the key Offices of EM. We recommend that steps be taken to ensure that user involvement in the focus areas is sufficient (and has sufficient expertise) to influence the early selection of technologies for development.

DECISION PROCESS FOR SELECTING CANDIDATE TECHNOLOGIES FOR DEVELOPMENT

The subcommittee is aware that EM is developing a decision-making framework that could potentially be used to select technologies for development by EM. We support the refinement of this framework and its eventual acceptance and use by the focus areas. The lack of an accepted and consistently applied framework is a distinct problem.

The framework must clearly identify who has the responsibility and authority to ask, answer, and make appropriate decisions regarding such fundamental technology-selection questions as the following:

• Is new technology needed to solve a given problem?

• Is technology that can adequately solve the problem available or under development (either inside or outside the Department)?

• If not, has the technical or scientific basis of any potential new technology that is being proposed been adequately demonstrated (theoretically or, better, experimentally)?

• Does the proposed new technology address a priority Department need that has been identified by a potential technology user or stakeholder (either at one site or at multiple sites)?

• How does the technology compare with other technologies that have been or are being developed elsewhere (including outside the Department complex)?

• Is there a compelling reason (i.e., related to potential for success, cost, ability to solve a difficult problem, etc.) why the Department (rather than someone else) should pursue development of the technology?

In addition, the framework needs to have an explicit link between the proposed technology development and customer needs as stated above.

The subcommittee recommends that the responsible person or entity for technology selection be clearly identified and that a knowledgeable peer-review group (which is independent and includes members from outside the Department, as discussed above) have substantial influence in the selection decision.

Because new technologies are constantly being developed, the decision-making framework must recognize that technology selection for the Department is a dynamic process that must be periodically revisited. Understanding of what kinds of technology are becoming available, not only from inside the Department but also from outside, is necessary.

Circumstances that must be accounted for in making technology-selection decisions change (e.g., funding levels may decline, the understanding of the health effects of different circumstances in the DOE complex may change, and the consequence for the environment may be better appreciated), so technology-selection decisions should be made with a view to achieving a strategic mix of technology developments that have short-term and longer-term payoffs.

TECHNOLOGY-DEVELOPMENT MODEL

The strategy of organizing EM technology development within focus areas offers the opportunity for radical redesign of procedures for development of new environmental-remediation technologies. To achieve optimal return from the new approach, a much-needed and fundamental paradigm shift for the EM technology-development program, a progressive conceptual model must be developed to guide and manage the process. Each focus area will have some special features and requirements, but the basic elements of the model will be more similar than different for the different focus areas. A model that divides technology-development projects into six categories or "gates" with screening criteria was discussed at the workshop. Gate 1 is the entrance for applied research, gate 2 is the entrance for exploratory development, gate 3 is the entrance for advanced development, gate 4 is the entrance for engineering development, gate 5 is the entrance for demonstration, and gate 6 is the entrance for implementation (see Figure 1).

Several specific requirements of the EM technology maturation model identified by the subcommittee should strengthen the EM technology-development effort.

Models for technology development must be strongly coupled to supporting research and development and to technology demonstration and utilization programs. That might be difficult to accomplish, considering the varied nature and dispersed organization of the research supported by the Department that is applicable to technology development. For example, the subsurface-science research program is not in EM, and most of the environmental-process research in EM is not in the Office of Technology Development. Nevertheless, because most new environmental-restoration technologies in several of the focus areas have their origins and underpinnings in environmental-process research (e.g., in transport, fate, and subsurface characteristics), a carefully nurtured, interactive relationship must be established between basic and applied research and technology development.

EM has recently begun an effort to coordinate its technology-development efforts with the Office of Energy Research, which houses much of the Department's basic research and is the principal office for interaction with nondefense Department National Laboratories. The Congress has allocated $50 million of EM Program funds for this effort. This type of linkage, including the defense-related Laboratories, where much of the expertise in nuclear materials resides, is precisely what is called for by this subcommittee. The Department should extend this attempt to create partnerships to include the basic-research efforts in universities and industrial concerns that are developing technology or undertaking their own research.

As with any program initiative in the Department that involves many groups with their own programmatic objectives (e.g., basic research in support of the Department's missions versus applied research for specific projects), it can be difficult to create an effective link between basic research and the needs of a specific program, such as the EM Program. A principal challenge to its success will be to convince all those who have managerial responsibility for the different groups that this shared initiative deserves their support and encouragement. The Department should provide incentives to its managers, Laboratories, and contractors to make initiatives like this a success.

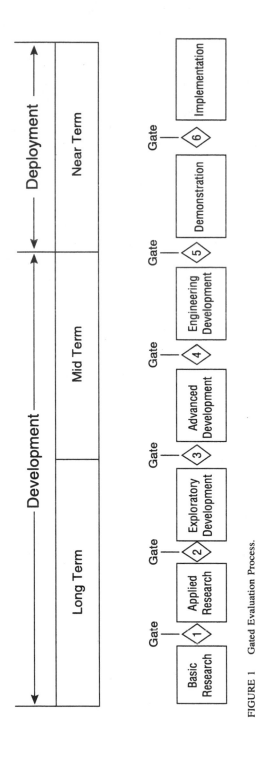

FIGURE 1   Gated Evaluation Process.

SOURCE: Gretchen McCabe, Battelle. Presentation at the National Academy of Sciences, July 12, 1995.

A way must be found to empower environmental-technology users to participate effectively in the allocation of applied-research and technology-development funding, regardless of the source in the Department.

Technology development must be tightly coupled to technology demonstration and user implementation if the barriers to the introduction of new technology are to be overcome. A mechanism that has proved effective in overcoming a number of barriers is stakeholder involvement from technology selection through all stages of development to final implementation. *Stakeholder* must also be broadly defined and include not only R&D and user personnel, but regulators at all levels, permit writers, and the public.

As emphasized above, a productive technology-development model must also be based on clearly articulated goals and analyses to determine whether the goals are likely to be achieved. Analyses should be included at multiple points in the development process to justify continued investment. Life-cycle costs of technologies in development should be subjected to economic analysis, and the potential risk reduction likely to result from the technology should be analyzed before huge sums are invested.

Cost analyses must be benchmarked against available technologies or other technologies under development, regardless of the sponsor. That will require EM to improve its research and technology-development outreach by opening the Department's R&D program to all qualified persons and organizations, regardless of type or location.

The subcommittee believes that technology-development funds should be awarded on a competitive basis. Creative partnerships between industry, academe, and National Laboratories should be encouraged.

Many of the Department's waste-management issues are not peculiar to the Department; they are faced by private industries and the Department of Defense as well. The Department should make full use of the expertise and talent in universities, industry, and other federal agencies. The role of industry and universities should be of several kinds:

- External peer review.
- Collaboration in technology development.
- Primary participation in technology development.

As with the technology-selection process, development should incorporate a broad-based system of peer review that is carefully implemented and monitored to ensure equity.

A system of incentives must be developed to increase the likelihood that new technologies will be implemented. Stakeholder involvement will help, but other approaches should be considered such as grants to communities that cooperate in the demonstration of new technologies.

COST-BENEFIT ANALYSIS AS PART OF THE TECHNOLOGY-DEVELOPMENT PROCESS

Calculation of costs and benefits takes into account a number of factors. Costs should include life-cycle costs, as well as shorter-term costs. Life-cycle cost is an estimate of the full cost of implementing the technology over its expected life; estimation uses a discounted present value analysis (in its most useful form, a range of interest rates, including 0.0%, are used). This allows comparison of short-term capital intensive technologies with longer-term, more cost-effective technologies on an equal basis. Examples of benefits are: decreased likelihood that contamination will reach or affect a population, increased reliability of the method for containing pollution or remediating, decreased production of secondary waste, increasing safety for workers in the environmental management program, and development of a method that might have wide use or commercial viability. As with any analytical tool of this kind, life-cycle analysis has its critics. DOE should use it with this in mind, be certain to make clear statements about the assumptions used, and seek participation of stakeholders in making judgments about these assumptions.

Cost-benefit analysis should be included at each step of the research and technology-development process in the Department. Obviously, the proof of effectiveness should be much less stringent and detailed for basic and applied research and for exploratory development than would be required for more-advanced stages of technology development.

The technology-development model with screening criteria was presented at the workshop by Gretchen McCabe of Battelle (see Figure 1, above). The general approach embodied in the screening criteria was supported by the subcommittee. Although many variants of this model are possible, it serves the purpose of making a few general points. In the model presented, cost-benefit analysis is used to determine whether a project passes the fourth gate from "advanced development" to "engineering development," which involves prototype development and testing. Incorporation of cost-benefit analysis at this stage in the process is appropriate, but as stated above, it should be applied throughout the process and with different levels of detail, depending on the uncertainties associated with the particular stage of development.

The level of detail required for cost-benefit analysis is different at different levels of technology development. For projects in the basic-research, applied-research, or exploratory-development stage, there should be a description of scientific reasons for expecting costs to be reduced if the project is developed and of benefits (with respect to risk reduction, cleanup time, and reduction of secondary wastes) that can be expected if the project is successful. The scientific basis for expecting specific benefits needs to be explained. The issues that will substantially affect costs and benefits should be identified as early as possible in the technology-development process.

For more-advanced projects (gates 4, 5, and 6), the level of detail about costs and benefits should be increased. Claims of cost savings or benefits should be documented. At this point, information on the expected implementation of the technology should be sufficient for estimating the life-cycle cost for some generic or site-specific examples. It should also allow estimation of hidden implementation costs. In the assessment of these more-mature projects (gates 4–6), specific cost-benefit goals should be stated; e.g., a working target might be to remove cadmium from soil at a cost 20% less than the cost of current landfill solutions or to remove a contaminant from groundwater at a rate 30% faster and at no higher cost than a current-pump-and-treat strategy. The decision to fund further technology-development projects will be based in part on the stated goals and the ability of the projects to meet goals declared at earlier gates. There should be at all stages a comparison of the costs and benefits of using the new technology and established technologies for the same pollution problem.

For example, aquifer characteristics, such as hydraulic conductivity might be known to have a major effect on the feasibility and cost of a particular bioremediation technology. Hydraulic conductivity is a measure of how easily water moves through soil; it varies widely between soil types. In this example, proposals for bioremediation programs in the early stages (e.g., research or exploratory development) should identify this important property of soils and discuss how the issue will be considered in the analysis. Proposals for more advanced work (advanced or engineering development and beyond) should be able to measure the impact of hydraulic conductivity on feasibility and cost. In addition, consideration of the applicability of a particular technology should include a discussion of the impact of this factor (e.g., how large the market for this type of technology is, given the conductivity requirements). For most projects, several such issues need to be identified early in development and continually revisited with increasingly detailed analysis as the technology passes through the various gates.

Peer reviewers should have information about the costs and benefits of a technology project in comparison with those of other existing technologies to assist them in their evaluations.

ROLE OF THE NATIONAL LABORATORIES
IN TECHNOLOGY DEVELOPMENT

The decision as to whether National Laboratories, universities, or industry should take the lead in the development of any particular technology should be based on a competitive process that undergoes external review, not on a formula or some other form of entitlement. Often, teaming together and partnering different groups for the development of a particular technology is the most effective approach.

National Laboratories constitute an extraordinary technical resource in both capability and size. It must be recognized, however, that they are unique in culture and expertise (especially with nuclear materials); this can be both an advantage and a disadvantage in bringing new technologies to bear in restoration activities. There must be strong external benchmarking and peer review of research and technology-development efforts in National Laboratories. The Laboratories must be open to procurement of "outside" capabilities even when the main body of the R&D fits inside. As with all participants in the technology-development effort, a Laboratory should structure efforts to be responsive to the technology customers.

Experience has demonstrated time and again that the National Laboratories are most effective at producing technologies that have potential for commercialization when they are linked to industry at the earliest possible time. The idea is for industry to provide "technology pull" that can guide R&D so that a product meets customer requirements and there are no surprises when it is turned over to industry for commercialization.

Partnerships between industry, the Laboratories, and universities in which each party contributes what it does best may be desirable.[4] The National Laboratories, for example, have extraordinary expertise in simulation and modeling, advanced materials, chemistry, fluid dynamics, and other disciplines of potential interest to industry. Furthermore, the Laboratories have officially designated user facilities—usually one-of-a-kind instruments or Laboratories that are available for industrial collaboration with a minimum of paperwork and bureaucracy.

Other models for technology development have not been very successful. Technologies that are developed without industry participation face a much more difficult road to commercialization for a variety of reasons, ranging from difficulty of manufacture to the "not invented here" syndrome where a company is not interested in developing a technology because it had nothing to do with its earliest development.

---

[4]An example of this partnership model is developing at the Los Alamos National Laboratory. In early 1995, Motorola approached the Laboratory about developing technologies for cleanup of solvent-contaminated groundwater. Motorola visited the Laboratory on several occasions to inform Laboratory scientists and engineers of the customer requirements, including providing information on the extent of the problem and possible approaches that would be acceptable in the existing corporate and regulatory environment. The Laboratory plans to allocate some of its FY 1996 laboratory-directed research and development funds to start a small number of projects that will be conducted with expanded industry involvement, including that of Motorola and other interested companies. If promising solutions can be developed during the coming year, Motorola has agreed to lead a program-development effort for continued funding.

Technology Utilization

The magnitude and diversity of Department waste-management problems dictate that there be a hierarchy of approaches to deciding where and when technologies are used or developed. The hierarchy should apply even within a technology-selection process like that described above. These approaches can be categorized according to the nature of the remediation activity as

• Technologies related to interim waste-management measures, such as those needed to maintain burial grounds, existing facilities, waste repositories, and plant-waste treatment systems until a final remediation option is agreed on and effected.

• Technologies related to final remediation of wastes, such as those needed for processing waste-tank contents, producing final waste forms, and decontaminating and decommissioning equipment and facilities. It is important to note here that the EM Program must define final waste forms in collaboration with the Office of Civilian Radioactive Waste Disposal if it is to guide the development of these technologies properly.

• Technologies needed in connection with custodial activities, including a wide spectrum of instrumentation for monitoring and isolating sites that must still be retained by the Department.

Which technology approach to pursue will be determined by which goals (such as land use and cleanup levels) are selected and what level of priority a particular site or remediation activity receives on the basis of the magnitude of associated risks and cost-benefit rating.

There are several ways to obtain technologies. The best approach will

123

depend upon whether the problem is peculiar to Department sites, is not peculiar to Department sites but poses a need for improved technologies and processes for remediation, or can be solved with existing technologies supplied by private companies.

It is important to establish an explicit policy to encourage private-company participation in solving problems in the first two categories. Successful participation in the first category will mean that the waste-management experience of the private sector will be shared and market-driven management principles will be brought to the problem. In the second category, involvement of the private sector might lead to the development of a process or technology that gains broader commercial-market acceptance.

For private companies to enter the technology market for Department waste problems successfully, they must have or develop an adequate and secure financial base, a facility for manufacturing and distributing equipment, and a good understanding of the regulatory and liability aspects of doing business with the Department. If any of those requirements are missing, the Department should be prepared to assist the companies if it finds the technology desirable. The technology must be both "robust" and safe. In all procurement approaches, there must be provisions for testing and validation of technologies in real-world conditions. The possibility of failure to meet target criteria or goals must be accommodated without excessive penalties. In fact, what is learned from failure can sometimes be as valuable as success would have been. The Department should indemnify a technology developer during test and demonstration against an unplanned contamination of the environment, but not against failure to properly perform the work. The site operator and the local stakeholders who have taken risks in deciding to use innovative technology should be rewarded, not penalized, if the technology fails.

When the point is reached where technology procurement is required it is essential that the responsible, knowledgeable people at the individual sites be intimately involved in defining the bounds of the problem. It is necessary to have trained, experienced, competent people; support organizations to ensure the health and safety of personnel; and management and maintenance functions to sustain the site infrastructure. In most cases, the site-operating contractor must retain the right of final approval of the proposed technology, to the extent that it can ensure the health and safety of people both on the site and in the community around the site, so that it can ensure preservation of its investment in the site.

Technologies exist both in the Department complex and in private industry to deal with many of the Department's waste problems. Some problems, however, are so complex that there is no identifiable technological solution. A possible way to deal with such problems is to break them into smaller problems. That creates a requirement for important systems analyses and technology-interface studies before decisions on technology procurement can be made.

It is especially important that narrowly defined solutions to individual problems not create or exacerbate other problems. For example, technologies for treating Hanford tank wastes might very well remove wastes from the tanks, but the resulting product streams could be very expensive to vitrify or could lead to excessive volumes of waste. It is critical to consider the waste problem and its solution broadly enough for the solution chosen to deal effectively and acceptably with the whole problem in a systems context. It does little to solve the Hanford tank-waste problem (although it may help some in reducing worker risks) by emptying the tanks to within 99% of total cleanup if there has been significant leakage from the tanks already into the surrounding soil. In a case like that, barrier technology to isolate the tank farm might be preferable to technology for cleaning out the tanks and separating the waste constituents for individual disposal.

References

Blush, Steven M. and Thomas H. Heitman. 1995 Train Wreck Along the River of Money: an Evaluation of the Hanford Cleanup, A Report for the U.S. Senate Committee on Energy and Natural Resources, Washington, D.C.

DOE (U.S. Department of Energy). 1994. A New Approach to Environmental Research and Technology Development at the Department of Energy: Action Plan. U.S. Department of Energy Office of Environmental Management, Washington, D.C.

DOE (U.S. Department of Energy). 1995a. Closing the Circle on the Splitting of the Atom: The Environmental Legacy of Nuclear Weapons Production in the United States and What the Department of Energy is Doing About It. The U.S. Department of Energy, Office of Environmental Management, Office of Strategic Planning and Analysis (EM-4), Washington, D.C.

DOE (U.S. Department of Energy). 1995b. Estimating the Cold War Mortgage: The 1995 Baseline Environmental Management Report. Volume I, March 1995. U.S. Department of Energy Office of Environmental Management, Washington, D.C.

DOE (U.S. Department of Energy). 1995c. Environmental Management 1995: Progress and Plans of the Environmental Management Program. The U.S. Department of Energy, Office of Environmental Management, Washington, D.C.

DOE (U.S. Department of Energy). 1995d. Risks and the Risk Debate: Searching for Common Ground "The First Step". The U.S. Department of Energy, Office of Environmental Management, Washington, D.C.

DOE (U.S. Department of Energy). 1995e. Alternative Futures for the Department of Energy Laboratories. The U.S. Department of Energy, Secretary of Energy Advisory Board, Washington, D.C.

NRC (National Research Council). 1994. Building Consensus Through Risk Assessment and Risk Management in the Department of Energy's Environmental Remediation Program. National Research Council, Washington, D.C.

NRC (National Research Council). 1995. Committee on Environmental Management Technologies: Report for the Period Ending December 31, 1994. National Research Council, Washington, D.C.

OTA (U.S. Congress, Office of Technology Assessment). 1991. Complex Cleanup: The Environmental Legacy of Nuclear Weapons Production. OTA-O484. U.S. Government Printing Office, Washington, D.C.

Parker, Frank L. Statement of Frank L. Parker, Distinguished Professor of Environmental Engineering, Vanderbilt University, Westinghouse Distinguished Scientist Professor of Environmental Systems Engineering, Clemson University. Senate Committee on Environment and Public Works, Sub-Committee on Superfund Waste Control and Risk Assessment. May 9, 1995.

Appendix
PREVIOUS STUDIES

The titles and brief summaries of many of the studies on improving technology development follow.

1. *Status and Analysis of Environmental Technology Management at DOE*, October 1994. The report summarizes major observations made in analyzing the technology-development efforts of the Office of Waste Management, the Office of Environmental Restoration, and the Office of Technology Development and makes recommendations on the basis of some of these observations. Among the observations are the following: technology developers must recognize that environmental technology is needed now for field application to problems that pose a threat, industrial partners must be involved, most of the Department's technology-development efforts are directed toward the enhancement of existing technologies, and a considerable number of environmental technologies and services available in the private sector can be applied now to the Department's environmental-restoration needs. The Department is implementing a new approach to environmental technology and development that will correct some of the conditions observed. The new structure is aimed at reducing redundancy, increasing communication, and coordinating and streamlining the process of technology development and management better.

2. *Barriers to Environmental Technology Commercialization*, Environmental Management Advisory Board, Technology Development and Transfer Subcommittee, April 1995. The subcommittee categorized the numerous complex

barriers into two broad groups: primary barriers, which the Department can influence substantially; and secondary barriers, which are more generic. Examples of identified primary barriers are lack of adequate Department-site characterizations, insufficient technology performance or cost data, and cumbersome Department contracting and procurement requirements. Examples of identified secondary barriers are lack of entrepreneurial management, lack of adequate development funding, lack of consistent regulatory enforcement, and limited technology applications for the private sector. Some of the secondary barriers are acknowledged to be outside the realm of the Department. The subcommittee also acknowledges that developing new environmental technologies to reach the marketplace is a battle. The subcommittee recommends the acceleration of assessments of Department-site contamination to provide faster definition of technology and market needs, strengthening of the linkage between technology development and technology deployment, and continuation of aggressive collaborative efforts with EPA and states to resolve or reduce major impediments to permitting.

3. *Committee on Environmental Management Technologies Report for the Period Ending December 31, 1994*, NRC, Board on Radioactive Waste Management, Commission on Geosciences, Environment, and Resources, 1995. The first report of this committee supports EM's attempts to find generic solutions to major environmental problems through integration of the activities of EM-30, EM-40, EM-50, and EM-60 and encourages EM to continue to focus R&D efforts on clearly identified problems. The committee also recommends the development of new technologies as backups to current technologies.

4. *Federal Environmental Research and Development*, Carnegie Commission on Science, Technology, and Government, 1992. The report recognizes that the federal government generally lacks a coordinated approach toward environmental R&D. That lack makes it difficult to establish budget priorities and conduct efficient and effective research.

5. *Preparing for the Future Through Science and Technology: An Agenda for Environmental and Natural Resources*, National Science and Technology Council, Committee on Environment and Natural Resources, March 1995. The report divides research in the areas of toxic substances and wastes into risk assessment and risk management (pollution prevention, controls, remediation, and monitoring). Subjects of "enhanced emphasis" named in the report include improving risk-assessment capabilities and improving risk-management tools. The report emphasizes the need for developing more cost-effective means of remediating short-term environmental problems. The report recommends accelerating the diffusion of new technologies into the marketplace through partnerships with industry, state and local governments, academe, and nongovernment organizations.

6. *Report of the Defense Science Board Task Force on Environmental Security*, Department of Defense, Office of the Under Secretary of Defense, Acquisition and Technology, April 1995. The DOD environmental-remediation effort costs billions of dollars per year. Among the subjects for improvement that the report addresses is accelerating environmental-technology development and deployment. It notes that many existing technologies offer risk-reduction and cost-reduction potentials that are not being realized, partly because of regulatory barriers. It identifies the barriers to deployment of new environmental technology as forming the most serious bottleneck and expresses concern that with today's shrinking environmental budgets, investments in environmental science and technology that could substantially reduce future costs will not be made. The group made several recommendations for accelerating technology development and deployment. Among them are devoting an additional $150 million per year for accelerated environmental-technology demonstration and verification, making assignment of responsibility clear, developing a set of incentives for federal-site directors to use new technologies, and expanding cooperation among agencies and with industry.

7. *Alternative Futures for the Department of Energy Laboratories*, February 1995. Secretary of Energy Advisory Board, Chapter III, "The Energy, Environment, and Related Sciences and Engineering Role." This report, also known as the Galvin report, examines the role of the Department's National Laboratories. This section reviewed the Department's EM Program and addressed the Laboratories' energy and environmental roles and strongly criticized the EM Program. One of the most important challenges facing the Department and its Laboratories, as noted in the report, is to achieve greater integration of its various applied and fundamental energy R&D programs. Many facets of research and technology development constitute the appropriate energy agenda for the Laboratories.

8. *Management Changes Needed to Expand Use of Innovative Cleanup Technologies*, U.S. General Accounting Office, August 1994. The report identifies internal and external barriers to the use of new environmental technologies. It notes that although the Department has spent a large amount to develop waste-cleanup technology, little new technology is being incorporated into the agency's cleanup actions. Part of the agency's problem, the report notes, is that the Department does not have a well-coordinated and fully integrated technology-development program. The Department's plan to restructure its technology development programs is a step toward alleviating these problems. In addition, field offices will consider new and innovative technologies more seriously.

9. *Cleaning Up the Department of Energy's Nuclear Weapons Complex*, Congressional Budget Office, May 1994. The report outlines the Department's environmental problems and its cleanup program, including such policy issues as understanding risks, weighing costs and benefits, setting priorities, and

investing in the development of better technologies. The report acknowledges that the Department's cleanup program must address a problem that was created and largely ignored over the last 50 years. The Department is faced with addressing that problem during an especially tight budget climate. The report suggests that understanding of risks and costs better would be the best way to determine priorities for allocating scarce cleanup funds. It recommends investing more heavily in technology development, delaying technically difficult projects, and cutting overhead costs to improve the efficiency of cleanup efforts. In addition, new management systems might help the Department and Congress track the performance of cleanup projects.

Part V
Integration of Science, Engineering, and Health in Program Implementation

SUBCOMMITTEE ON INTEGRATION OF SCIENCE, ENGINEERING, AND HEALTH IN PROGRAM IMPLEMENTATION

VICTORIA J. TSCHINKEL (*Chair*), Senior Consultant on Environmental Issues, Landers & Parsons

BETSY ANCKER-JOHNSON, Vice President of Environmental Activities (retired), General Motors Corporation

PHILIP H. BRODSKY, Director, Corporate Research and Environmental Technology, Monsanto Company

DAVID S.C. CHU, Director, Washington Research Department, RAND

BENJAMIN COSGROVE, Senior Vice President (retired), Boeing Commercial Airplane Group

BRIAN COSTNER, Director, Energy Research Foundation

ROBERT C. FORNEY, Executive Vice President (retired), E.I. du Pont de Nemours & Company

JAMES H. JOHNSON, JR., Professor and Acting Dean, School of Engineering, Howard University

MILDRED MCCLAIN, Executive Director, Citizens for Environmental Justice

BERNICE K. MCINTYRE, President, B.K.McIntyre & Associates, Inc.

MAXINE L. SAVITZ, General Manager, Ceramic Components, Allied Signal Aerospace Company

Staff

Tamae Maeda Wong, Senior Program Officer
Helen Chin, Administrative Assistant

Introduction

The subcommittee held a 1.5-day workshop on August 29 and 30, 1995, to meet with representatives of industry, Department of Energy (DOE) Environmental Management (EM) Program officials, Department of Defense (DOD) officials, and personnel from Department of Energy contractors. The subcommittee was impressed by the degree to which the Department of Energy has recognized many of the key issues inhibiting the success of the EM Program. The Subcommittee identified and directed its attention to four subjects which would be most helpful in improving the integration of science, technology, and engineering into the EM Program:

• *The Department's management system, including its relationship to contractors and regulators.* The subcommittee noted that the organizational structure of DOE bifurcates responsibility for environmental management; thus decision-making and incentive-system processes are not optimally designed to help the EM Program meet its stated goals.

• *The management of remediation-related research and development and its relationship to the Department of Energy's field activities.* Needs-based research should be well coordinated and integrated into activities in the EM Program.

• *Environmental practices in industry.* Several subcommittee members have experience in this regard, and the subcommittee heard from industrial representatives. For most companies, cleanup is a necessary sideline: they must do it well, finish the job, and let the rest of the company focus on its core business. Industrial cleanup has a well-defined objective. In the Department, the EM Program faces many long-term challenges and the program could easily be plagued by inefficiency if it becomes a self-perpetuating entity that is not managed carefully to attain its many independent goals (with completion of site remediation being just one among many).

• *The relationship between scientific and technical information and effective public participation.* Better communication and more meaningful, timely opportunities for public involvement are needed.

As the subcommittee focused on those subjects, it kept in mind the Department of Energy's stated goals of protection of public health and the environment, compliance with all regulatory requirements, efficiency, and cost-effectiveness. The subcommittee was struck by the difficulty faced by the Department in trying to establish and manage a program that must operate over several decades, especially in light of changing political leadership and congressional decisions. It also recognized the crucial inter-relationship between good management practices and the ability to integrate science and technology into decision-making. That led it to several recommendations for identifying the best business practices to create a climate for integration. In developing the recommendations, it acknowledged several factors that distinguish the Department's EM Program from private industry and therefore affect the agency's ability to adopt a business model fully, including the expectations of and demands on a public agency, the Department's history of self-regulation and poor management practices, and especially the unique challenges posed by radioactive waste and fissile materials.

The subcommittee was impressed with the degree to which the Department's leadership recognizes the need for improvement. The Department is currently in an active, transitional state, attempting to instill cultural and organizational change in the EM Program. Specifically, the EM Program is realigning its activities to meet the six goals set forth by Assistant Secretary Thomas Grumbly:

• Eliminate and manage urgent risks in the system.
• Emphasize health and safety for workers and the public.
• Establish a system that is managerially and financially in control.
• Demonstrate tangible results.
• Focus technology development on identifying and overcoming obstacles to progress.
• Establish a stronger partnership between the Department and its stakeholders.

One example of how the program is attempting to achieve its goals is the introduction of contract reform. Several basic elements of this reform are increased competition; renewed focus on the protection of workers, the public, and the environment; a results-oriented focus; and performance-based incentives.

In recent months, a performance based integrated contract adopting these elements of contract reform has been introduced and implemented at the Rocky Flats Environmental Technology Site in Colorado (*Independent Technical Review of Rocky Flats Program*, June 1995). Some workshop participants emphasized that it is too early to predict the effectiveness of the new contract, but subcommittee members strongly supported the intentions and direction of the contract-reform effort. The contract for the Savannah River Site in South Carolina is also being re-bid with several of the reform elements, but only the current contractor has opted to bid.

Other initiatives are rapidly introducing additional change into a system that was established during the Cold War. Some of the more notable efforts as previously discussed include integration of risk and long-term cost data into the budget process, addressing land-use planning at several Department sites, and realigning internal organizations. Although it is too early to assess how effective and long-lasting these efforts will be, the principles and general direction of reform are encouraging.

Internal Management and Contractor Relations

Some fundamental concepts must be addressed by any organization if it is to accomplish its stated goals. First, there must be effective leadership and a clear understanding by all involved about the goals of the organization, including its immediate and longer-term plans for accomplishing them. Next, an organizational structure must be established and management tools implemented to execute the plans and accomplish the goals. The subcommittee approached its discussion of the integration of science, engineering, and health in the internal management and organization of the EM Program, by addressing the framework for management and contractor relations, namely: leadership, goals, products and services, management tools, management structure, and incentives and disincentives.

LEADERSHIP

Issue: The EM Program must have strong leadership and, when necessary, attention from the Secretary of Energy.

The key to good leadership is the empowerment of those within an organization to make and be responsible for decisions in a way that promotes the accomplishment of the organization's goals.

The EM Program uses more than one-third of the Department of Energy budget. The importance of the environmental activities and the high degree of community concern over the safety of Department facilities dictate that the Secretary of Energy take a leadership role, through personal involvement, on select issues for the EM Program. The present Secretary initiated such activities early in her term through active involvement with affected communities. It will be important, as the Department focuses on facility management policies, for the Secretary to lead the way in pursuing and maintaining active progress.

The Secretary, through her emphasis on total quality management, has sought to clearly assign responsibility for performance. However, the current reporting structure through two different lines of authority involving both the offices of Environmental Management and Field Management (see Management Structure section) makes it difficult to implement the necessary accountability within the Department. Clarification of lines of responsibility will promote identification of responsible managers and minimize the phenomenon known as "stovepiping" where different organizational units within the EM Program share responsibility yet have little communication. It should lead to improvements in the mechanisms for raising, considering, and resolving EM issues that cross organizational units and will help develop a more focused agenda for the EM Program.

Recommendations:

1. Clearly, one of the principal roles of the Secretary is in setting the Department's major environmental goals. She also has the responsibility for empowering Department staff to accomplish those goals, making cross-program decisions, and taking decisions that require coordination with other departments to the appropriate interagency forum or to the President. There is a need for continued and strengthened leadership by the Secretary.

2. An organizational structure that places responsibility for deciding and executing programmatic priorities as discussed under "Management Structure" would facilitate EM Program efforts to integrate its science, technology, and engineering needs and missions with those of the rest of the Department. DOE is making efforts in this direction. This organization chart should be structured to serve operational needs and should, when necessary, create functional teams to address cross-organizational issues. All operational activities should be within the control of line managers. (See also sections on Management Structure, subsection B, and Lessons from Industrial Management Programs, section IV.)

MANAGEMENT STRUCTURE

Issue: Bifurcated responsibility for EM activities unnecessarily complicate the reporting structure.

The lines of responsibility for the conduct of the EM Program are diffuse within the Department. The organization chart divides the responsibility for conducting the EM Program between the Associate Deputy Secretary for Field Management, who reports to the Deputy Secretary, and the Assistant Secretary for Environmental Management, who reports to the Undersecretary. Contract management and procurement is the responsibility of the Associate Deputy Secretary, and programmatic direction and budgeting is the responsibility of the Assistant Secretary for Environmental Management.

The field offices are at eight sites, including the five that consume 70% of the budget of the EM Program. According to the August 3, 1995, issue of the *EM Alignment Initiative Newsletter*, the Assistant Secretary for Environmental Management stated, "We are responsible for program development and program direction." The field is responsible for program execution. There are few mechanisms for the Assistant Secretary to hold the field accountable for implementing the EM Program's goals. Those who instigate an operation, such as the remediation of the high-level nuclear waste tanks at Hanford or a cleanup design, generally do not have responsibility to oversee the actual cleanup operation, because the contract operators do not report to the Assistant Secretary for EM. The responsibility loop apparently never closes in the existing structure until it reaches the Secretary's level.

Recommendation:

The line of responsibility for all environmental activities should be in one reporting structure within the Department with authority following the responsibility lines. This change would clarify accountability and facilitate integrated consideration of environmental activities. If the Department substituted a carefully crafted matrix organization, common in many corporations, bifurcation of management responsibility might work, although admittedly it is one of the most difficult organizational structures to make effective and must never be a substitute for clear lines of authority and responsibility.

Issue: The present organizational structure in the Office of the Assistant Secretary for EM has demarcations that prevents consideration of optimal system-wide solutions.

A waste tank and its contents, for example, might involve every major EM office, as well as other DOE offices. The waste could be generated by DOE's Office of Defense Programs or Nuclear Energy; EM's Office of Waste Management, Facility Transition, or Environmental Remediation; or another office entirely. The tank contents and its treatment, storage, and disposal would be managed by EM's Office of Waste Management. Response to a spill or leak could be handled by the site's emergency response team which might be operated out of different offices at various DOE sites. Disposition of the tank itself after emptying would likely be the responsibility of EM's Office of Environmental Remediation or Facility Transition. Any contaminated soil or groundwater associated with the tank and its contents would be the responsibility of EM's Office of Environmental Remediation. There are, unfortunately, few incentives or mechanisms to encourage systematic approaches involving multi-program teams, to manage the waste tank, its contents, and the surrounding environment.

Recommendation:

Environmental activities should be handled by teams that are organized around functional needs and site-specific programs. The introduction of organizational barriers that inhibit the application of good scientific principles should be avoided. A paradigm for consideration is the team approach used by industry. For example, teams may be composed of technical, legal, and financial managers. Depending on the stage of a project, the lead person for the project could be any one of those. The team can be supplemented by R&D, state government-relations, public-relations, real-estate, and construction personnel. That approach ensures a coordinated legal, technical, and financial strategy. The Office of Technology Development in DOE has recently established five Focus Areas in which to manage technology development and research on a team basis. That effort, in its initial stages, might demonstrate the utility of such a management approach, and lessons learned from it should be applied to the broad team concept suggested here.

GOALS

Often in government, middle- and lower-level staff lack a clear understanding of the ultimate purposes of the programs for whose execution they are responsible; a result is that outdated programs continue or dubious practices are continued on the feeble grounds that "we're just following orders" (from Congress, from higher officials, etc.). If the staff does understand the purposes of the programs at the outset, their understanding sometimes attenuates with time leading to similar results. To overcome that problem, the leadership of a department must constantly emphasize the importance of the department's goals. Successful departments ensure that discussions of work plans begin with a review of the goals that they serve. They encourage challenges to constraints that preclude achievement of those goals, including political constraints, and recognize that the political leadership within the department bears the responsibility for raising and debating these constraining issues with vigor.

Issue: Some goals of the EM Program are unstated, and these sometimes conflict with the stated goals.

This has complicated and slowed efforts to achieve the Department's long-term objectives for reducing risks to the public, workers, and the environment.

The stated goal of the cleanup is to reduce risk at the site quickly and efficiently. However, an often unstated goal is to provide continued employment and funding for the site. Organizational structures and decision-making by contractors and EM employees that would accelerate remediation or reduce the number of people required to carry it out could result in reduced employment or funding. Under the current system, states and local governments want to see rapid action toward achieving safer sites and safer operation of them, but they also want maximal employment at Department sites. Labor unions and contractors also benefit from larger and slower programs.

Recommendations:

1. All goals should be clearly identified, ranked, and communicated in writing, and the organizational structure should facilitate the achievement of those goals. The goals should be sufficiently defined to stand as milestones against which performance can be measured.

2. New incentive systems (for stakeholders, contractors, and workers) for rewarding better performance as measured against the goals should be explored.

3. States, tribal, and local governments should continue to be encouraged to participate in the EM planning and budget process so that they can become aware of and adapt to the budget pressures and other realities faced by the program.

PRODUCTS AND SERVICES

Once an organization has established its overall goals and the plans for achieving them, it can determine the activities or ''products and services'' that it will pursue day by day. Some are obvious and others are harder to define. In the case of the EM Program, remediation and waste-minimization activities are obviously essential for accomplishing the fundamental objective of the program.

Technology development, on the other hand, is an example of a product or service with a less well-defined role. Should the program pursue its own projects for the development of technology or leave decisions on technology development to the contractors that are carrying out the remediation effort? Should decisions about whether to pursue processes and technology for waste minimization throughout the Department's operations be made by the EM Program or left to the Offices of Energy Research and Defense Programs that operate the facilities? How such questions are answered will be affected by outside circumstances, such as the newly imposed financial restraint on the EM Program. The EM Program now hopes to reduce its expenditures by $10 billion for the period 1995–2000 through improvements in efficiency.

Issue: EM products and services are not fully defined, and changing external forces complicate efforts to define them.

The EM Program is still defining the less-obvious products that it should be producing (e.g., its technology development process). The EM Program is being forced to change its approach to its long-term goals because of appropriate demands for fiscal restraint and the ever-increasing pressure to accomplish its goals faster and more cost-effectively, and there is confusion as to what the near-term objectives of the program should be. For instance, does the technology development program exist to do basic research or to develop market-oriented technologies? The Department recognizes the need to identify technology gaps so that R&D can begin, but what constitutes a "gap" is not clear. Is the EM Program seeking to develop technology only as necessary for a particular waste minimization activity or environmental problem that currently has no solution? Is the goal to develop only technology that will reduce the cost or increase the speed of remediation activities? Or is it to reduce worker risks? Efforts to identify technology gaps in a coordinated agency-wide manner have resulted in a proliferation of reports, most of which have not provided a totally acceptable road map for action; e.g., *Hanford Integrated Planning Process: 1993 Hanford Site Specific Science and Technology Plan* (DOE, 1993a) and the *Technology Needs Crosswalk Report* (DOE, 1993b) were used only superficially after their publication.

A further problem that arises from the confusion is that without a clear understanding of what the Environmental Management Program needs to produce to meet its long-term goals, it is very difficult to determine program or employee productivity.

Recommendations:

1. EM, in revisiting its goal-setting process, should determine what services or products it must deliver, and establish goals that reflect the new budget pressures. The goals must be sufficiently detailed to lessen confusion about how to design products and services to attain them.

2. To that end, the EM Program should continue to "benchmark" itself against industry. It might want to benchmark against the electric-utility and telephone industries which are in the midst of redefining services in a more cost-conscious environment.

MANAGEMENT TOOLS

Former Secretary of Energy James Watkins wrote to the subcommittee that "there are as many philosophies of organization and management as there are managers." Similarly, there are many tools for implementing a given management scheme. The subcommittee has focused on a few tools that could be helpful to the EM Program. Some are already being used. EM recognizes that its costs and time to reach milestones are excessive and is to be commended for beginning a process of benchmarking and using private-sector advisers to review its activities (see, for example, *DOE February Benchmarking Meeting and Independent Technical Review of Three Waste Minimization and Management Programs*, August 1995).

Issue: New Roles for EM staff require new skills.

In the past, the Department has relied on a system of relatively independent national laboratories and defense production facilities to accomplish its research and defense missions. With the new challenge of technically difficult and expensive environmental activities, the Department has begun to look at new models for managing this effort. The EM Program is rebidding over $27 billion in contracts and renegotiating another $13.5 billion. Federal employees in the EM Program will need new technical and managerial skills, especially in the oversight of performance-based contracts, in contrast with the older cost-plus contracts.

Recommendations:

1. The managerial and technical needs of the EM Program should be analyzed to ensure that the Department and its current management and site operators have personnel skilled in negotiations to oversee their contracts. It might also be necessary for the EM Program to define and educate program and project managers about their roles in the administration of EM activities.

2. As discussed at the workshop, the Department might need to become more assertive in its dealings with contractors. A good institution for comparison might be the Department of Defense, where new contract and management activities for environmental programs have been implemented.

Issue: EM should complete the establishment of a priority-setting system.

Recommendations:

1. EM's priority-setting system must consider a wide range of factors, including risk. Elements that should be evaluated when considering risk include

- Immediacy of risk.
- Extent of risk to human health and the environment.
- Cost, availability, and effectiveness of existing technology.
- Likelihood of success, timing, cost, and effectiveness of new technologies.
- Community pressures for immediate actions.

2. The 1994 National Research Council Report *Ranking Hazardous-Waste Sites for Remedial Action* (NRC, 1994b) called for a unified national process of hazardous-waste site ranking to replace the current multiple approaches. In summarizing the report, the committee chair, Perry L. McCarty, said that "a single national process could provide a better basis for decisions about

priority setting, how much cleanup or containment should be undertaken at each site, and when.'' Any well-defined and substantiated process could assist EM in making such decisions within the Department complex, although admittedly, challenges will remain. EM should play a leadership role in developing a unified national process, but the implementation of such a procedure should not delay its own decision-making. Having said this, the subcommittee believes that many decisions, such as how much cleanup or containment should be undertaken at each site, should be the subject of interactive communications with the local stakeholders and regulators and consider site-specific information.

Issue: Unwieldy and irrelevant Department procedures often hamper potentially cost-effective and timely cleanup.

For example, samples collected during cleanup of a non-nuclear chemical spill at a nuclear production facility could not be shipped to an outside laboratory that did not have Nuclear Regulatory Commission licensing to handle uranium, even after measurements showed that the soil was not radioactive.

Recommendations:

1. More flexibility is warranted in the adoption of internal safety procedures that properly address the risks of particular operations and do not require use of "one size fits all" procedures that were designed for more-hazardous conditions.

2. The Department of Energy has correctly undertaken an extensive review of its internal regulatory orders; this review should continue. Similarly, the Secretary's establishment of the Advisory Committee on External Regulation of Department of Energy Nuclear Safety was an excellent step, and the findings of this group should be closely scrutinized by the administration and Congress.

Issue: The Department of Energy needs a sound, credible base of scientific and technical information.

Integration of science, engineering, and health in the implementation of the EM Program depends on the availability of scientific and technical information. Considerable attention has been paid to the need for more-complete, higher-quality, and independent scientific and technical information in other subcommittees' reports and in many reviews of the EM Program conducted since its inception in 1989 (NRC, 1994; OTA, 1991). The Department of Energy has attempted to respond by increasing the independence and credibility of, for example, radiation-related health research and risk assessment. In both of these areas, however, further improvements are needed. An example of this kind of an effort is the creation of the Consortium on

Risk Evaluation with Stakeholder Participation (CRESP), which resulted from recommendations of an earlier National Research Council report (NRC, 1994b), and has so far been successful.

Responsibility, including funding, for research on the health effects of operations in the nuclear weapons complex was held by the Department and its predecessor agencies until December 1990, when Secretary of Energy James Watkins signed a Memorandum of Understanding (MOU) with the Department of Health and Human Services (DHHS). That MOU transferred much of the responsibility for radiation-related health research to the DHHS and was widely hailed as an important step toward improving the quality and credibility of this research.

The importance of this effort to the EM Program is primarily that (1) providing independent answers to many questions about the consequences of past operations through dose-reconstruction projects, worker-health studies, and other health research is necessary to address public concerns, and (2) information about the extent of contamination, pathways, health effects, and other factors gleaned through these studies will become part of the information base on which future EM decisions rest.

Successful conduct of the research agenda depends on DOE funding and cooperation. Through the MOU cited above, DOE requests funds for studies and then transfers the funds to DHHS. DOE remains responsible for collecting most of the data used in the health research. Continuity of funding has been hindered by restraints on DOE: During the summer of 1995 when DOE responded to proposed cuts in its FY 1996 budget by substantially reducing the amount of money that it proposed to transfer. In response, DHHS put a several-month hold on much of the research program while it attempted to secure funding commitments from DOE. The existing MOU expires in December 1995, and details of an extension are being worked out.

Regarding risk assessment, after publication of the National Research Council report *Building Consensus Through Risk Assessment and Management of the Department of Energy's Environmental Remediation Program* (NRC, 1994a), DOE expanded its efforts to involve independent scientists from universities and private industry in efforts to evaluate risks within the EM Program. The two principal initial methods selected by DOE were a grant to the Consortium for Environmental Risk Evaluation, led by Tulane University and Xavier University, and the request for assistance through publication of a Notice of Program Interest, which resulted in an award to the Consortium for Risk Evaluation with Stakeholder Participation (CRESP) and four additional, smaller and shorter-term awards (UNLV, ASI, Cadmus, Phoenix). CRESP is mandated to lead the coordination effort among these awardees. Both methods reveal weaknesses in the EM Program's study of risk, such as data gaps, inconsistencies, and difficulties in comparing risks across programs (e.g., environmental remediation and nuclear-materials stabilization). Addressing those weaknesses will not be a simple or quick task.

Recommendation:

DOE should continue efforts to improve the independence, quality, and credibility of its scientific and technical information. That can be aided by providing greater assurance that DHHS will be able to continue to direct the radiation-related health research agenda by extending the MOU with provisions that try to guarantee stable funding. It can also be helped by further involvement of the public and independent scientists in reviews of risk and other information.

INCENTIVES AND DISINCENTIVES

Issue: Incentives for good performance by the Department are weak.

The internal operations of and the effectiveness of the integration of science and engineering into the EM Program are hampered by conflicting incentives that are unwritten but understood by employees. For instance, employees are instructed by their superiors that projects need to be completed within definite periods, but their experience tells them that a finished project can result in decreased funding for the program. Therefore, employees might try to ensure the survival of the program by being lax about deadlines. Their understanding of the political appointment process also can cause employees to ignore the chain of command because their civil service loyalties are more important for ensuring employment longevity. Such phenomena are generally parts of the culture of all organizations. However, it is necessary for the culture to support the stated goals of an organization to avoid employees' conflicting incentives that undermine management objectives.

Indeed, to the extent that budgets are allocated according to the extent and seriousness of the environmental problems faced by a site, in a perverse way liabilities become an asset. Likewise, with budgets tied to continuing containment and remediation processes, there is not as strong an incentive to complete projects as might be desired.

The poor incentive structure within the Department carried over to its major contracts until very recently. The Department of Energy is to be congratulated for moving toward performance-based contracts whenever it can, although additional measures will be needed to spur efficiency and to reward success, for both projects and individuals.

Recommendation:

Disincentives within the EM Program should be identified and eliminated so that EM goals and objectives can be reached.

Issue: Incentives for civil-service employees are inadequate.

Many people believe that civil-service regulations prohibit promotions without the addition of supervisory responsibilities, make it difficult to remove employees from positions for poor performance, and do not adequately reward employees for good performance.

It is possible to create a civil-service program that provides more incentives for good performance. Pilot programs of up to 5 years can be initiated by government agencies or units within the government. The National Institute for Standards and Technology had trouble in recruiting new scientists several years ago. It prepared and implemented the Personnel Demonstration Program to remove strict civil-service levels, offered some incentives, and was able to compete with industry for new employees. EM could pilot test a program that explores a different promotion, reward, and firing system. It could be modeled after successful industry and utility models. For example, in Allied Signal's Functional Excellence Review, employees within the bottom 5% for two appraisals are terminated. Employees performing well are reviewed on a regular basis and attempts are made to increase their responsibilities and mobility.

Recommendation:

EM should propose to the Office of Personnel Management and implement a pilot promotion, reward, and firing system.

Issue: New contracting methods will require a new structure.

Most major contracts in the EM Program have had the traditional Department cost-plus format. To its credit, DOE is implementing performance-based contracts. Well-defined, carefully negotiated performance-based contracts can confidently be expected to be much more cost-effective than cost-plus contracts.

Recommendations:

1. The movement toward performance-based contracts, rather than cost-plus contracts, is to be encouraged. However, as the Department moves toward performance-based contracting, lines of authority in the field will become further blurred between the Assistant Secretary for EM and the Associate Deputy Secretary for Field Management, compared with the previous practice of contracting for work on a cost-reimbursal basis. Responsibility for EM contracts let by DOE should reside fully within the EM Program. That would ensure closure of the open management loop described above in the Management Structure section. Experience shows that control under one line of management of all aspects of an operating contract for its duration is much more cost-effective than administration of contracts by multiple parallel lines of management. Using performance-based contracts should

require fewer Department of Energy personnel during the operating phase than are now employed.

2. Prior performance should be a key element in new contract awards.

Issue: EM must create incentives for contractors.

Recommendations:

1. The Department of Energy should become a leader in using incentives to motivate its constituent elements. It should consider the early implementation of the Government Performance and Results Act to emphasize performance metrics focused on outcomes and results.

2. The internal budgeting process and its administration should be revamped to reward site contractors that complete projects early and well. Where feasible, full funding of projects at their start should be considered as a reward for good performance (rather than basing budgets on estimated expenditures for the next fiscal year). Other examples of incentives may be to allow site contractors to retain at least some of whatever savings they achieve. Also, rewarding high-performing sites with new high-priority projects, rather than reducing funding upon successful completion of a project in a timely and cost-effective fashion, might increase productivity.

Integration of Science and Technology into the EM Program

Science and technology play a key role in virtually all the activities of EM. They help to determine priorities for site cleanup by providing the basis for sound risk assessments, provide the tools for achieving remediation goals, and provide the scientific rationale that reassures stakeholders that the priorities and actions of the Department are in their best interest. It is critical that the management structure of the Department be designed to identify and gain access to available technology in a timely and cost-effective fashion. The subcommittee believes that some specific advice on the management of technology development and the scientific research supporting the EM Program is in order.

For EM problems that lack good solutions, EM needs an effective way to bring its resources to bear by developing technologies. Good solutions must also be affordable relative to budget limits, and cost reduction should be an important criteria in new technology development. EM must also ensure that the technologies that have been developed are used and implemented effectively.

Issue: Scientific research and technology development for the EM Program must be tightly linked to the goals of those engaged in remediation and other waste and environmental management activities.

In the past, managers responsible for addressing unique problems have not had the authority to specify and acquire necessary technology rapidly, and managers responsible for handling common challenges have not had a forum to share resources and expertise fully. The current effort to remedy those situations through the formation of five "Focus Areas"—contaminant plume containment and remediation; mixed waste characterization, treatment, and disposal; high-level waste tank remediation; landfill stabilization; and decontamination and decommissioning—to address the most pressing problems is laudable. The focus group structure uses an implementation team for each subject to recommend the allocation of resources and to carry out research and development activities. Each team includes Department field representatives, stakeholders, regulators, and, most important, technology users.

Recommendation:
    The focus groups or any future organizational entities designed to bring users of science and technology closer to researchers and technology developers should have the ability to influence strongly the allocation of funds for EM research and technology development. That would align the budget more closely to the needs of field managers charged with execution of program activities to ensure that site-specific problems are solved.

Issue: The new Office of Science and Technology (OST) can contribute greatly to the accomplishment of EM goals, as can the DOE's Office of Energy Research (OER).
    Basic research might produce novel and cost-effective EM solutions.

Recommendation:
    The Assistant Secretary for EM should continue to work with the heads of OST and OER to identify technologies and longer-term research for solving EM problems in a holistic fashion. We applaud current efforts of OST to set aside a portion of its R&D budget for the use of OER for exploratory basic research.

Issue: Researchers and technology developers must not only be closely linked with the users of their work, but also be part of an overall systems approach to EM.
    Some processes and technologies that might adequately resolve a "crisis of the moment" might make remediation actions in the future far more difficult to implement. For example, in-situ vitrification of wastes could make further waste-reduction efforts more complex, and removal of liquids from buried tanks could make later slurrying of sediments more difficult.

Recommendation:
    All technical solutions should be evaluated in the light of further action that might be warranted at the site and in the context of a systems approach to the achievement of the Department's overall objectives.

Lessons from Industrial Environmental Management Programs

Progress in environmental management has been achieved by industrial corporations, as well as federal agencies. Some federal agencies are now comparing their processes for achieving environmental goals with those of industry, using, for example, benchmarking. To determine "best practices" and define "conduct of business," several industrial models were examined at the subcommittee's workshop.

Issue: Best business practices are not always being applied to the EM Program.

The EM Program has identified places where the effectiveness of its efforts could be improved by the use of management practices developed and used in the private sector. The subcommittee applauds that approach, and it is a useful and appropriate course for the Department and the EM Program in general to follow to ensure that science, technology, and engineering are integrated into its goals for protecting human health and the environment. In particular, the Department is beginning to use performance-based contracting and is even considering complete privatization of waste-remediation processes and technologies.

Recommendation:

In general, the subcommittee strongly supports these efforts. Fully implement best business practices to achieve substantial cost, schedule, and technologic benefits.

Issue: Industry manages its contracts intensively; the Department seems ambivalent about whether it is a "customer" or a "manager."

Some of the comments of EM managers who spoke to the subcommittee indicated that the Department must focus on becoming a better customer of services provided by its contractors or other external entities, rather than on managing the process. The belief that there is a choice is probably naive. It is more accurate to say that the EM Program needs to shift its emphasis away from micromanagement and toward negotiation and management of performance-based contracts that hold contractors accountable for their performance, not their process.

Recommendations:

1. The Department should be an informed consumer. Contractors should be selected with assurance that the best people will be assigned, that contacts and line-of-command are clear, and that negotiated prices are fair to the government and to the contractor.

2. Contracts should be carefully written with milestones that are appropriately selected at key points in the effort, and the Department should be vigilant to ensure that interventions between the milestones are kept to a minimum to prevent cost overruns.

Issue: Some constraints that industry does not face will continue to apply to the government.

The application of private-sector models to public-sector mandates is limited. For instance, if privatization as it is being considered is adopted by EM for portions of the Hanford remediation projects, the financial markets might be unwilling to shift the magnitude of risk involved to the private sector. That could mean that there would be no private-sector bidders to EM to take on the privatized program. If there are no bidders, smaller increments of the task—such as design, construction, or operation—should be put out for bids. Some tasks for privatization might have to be fully government financed or be the recipient of loan guarantees. Furthermore, even if the financial markets are willing to fund these undertakings, the public might challenge the privatized entities' solutions to remediation problems and hamper or stop implementation.

As stated earlier, the Department needs to learn to be a wise contract manager and not micromanage. However, the subcommittee recognizes that the Department will have to continue to take an active position to involve the public and respond to community concerns.

Recommendations:

1. In general, the Department's EM Program should use private-sector models and privatization to meet its objective. However, the models must

be carefully adapted to suit the public-sector mandates. For instance, if privatization is selected by the EM Program to accomplish its goals, the Department must recognize that it might have to supply mechanisms to encourage privatization, for example, guaranteeing in part a stream of revenue or permitting non-DOE customers to use the services of the selected contractor in order to obtain bidders.

2. The EM Program might have to create mechanisms to be responsive to the public, regardless of contractual relationships. That does not have to lead to micromanagement; it might require clearer performance standards or different contractual terms that do not depend on normal contractual remedies for breach of contract.

Issue: Industry is motivated to have an efficient cleanup operation.

Cleanup operations lie outside industries' core business and are paid for from the profits of that business. Therefore, their programs are designed to be very cost-effective. For example, entire technology strategies have been designed to minimize costs and risks at industrial sites by employing conventional technologies, ex situ processes, in situ processes, and natural restoration. Incentives can be offered to work units that perform effectively and efficiently. It can be argued that the EM Program, principally in its cleanup business, might not have incentives to be out of business quickly and efficiently.

Recommendation:

The government should develop a system to reward effective completion of cleanup projects.

Issue: Industry relies on multifunctional teams to manage cleanup projects.

Teams for projects can supplement the normal organizational structure. In industry, input by a multifunctional team—consisting of a technical project leader, a lawyer, a finance manager, a corporate researcher, government relations personnel, and real-estate and construction personnel—starts at the beginning of a project and continues through completion, with the leadership of the team and its composition changing as needs change. Teams, in many industries, are strongly supported by corporate leadership. Teams are usually most effective if there has been training throughout the organization in the operation and use of teams. The Department has been training some teams, but it is not clear at what level they are being used and whether they are multifunctional.

Recommendation:

EM should establish and train multifunctional teams for appropriate projects and empower them to manage the cleanup process. Clear lines of authority and responsibility must be established and maintained for effective team operations.

Integration of Science and Technology into the Community-Relations Process

The Department has made public, or stakeholder, involvement a high priority for the EM Program. Indeed, improving relations with people concerned about environmental activities at Department sites is one of Assistant Secretary Grumbly's six goals for the program. The quantity of available information and the opportunities for public involvement have increased substantially in recent years to meet that goal. In addition, the Department of Energy has put increased emphasis on incorporation of public involvement in the duties of program and project managers.

Public involvement is still evolving, and many of the participants—among the Department and its contractors, as well as within concerned and affected communities—continue to learn and adapt to the changes. One activity in which substantial improvements are needed is the integration of scientific and technical information.

Issue: The Department of Energy needs to communicate information more effectively.

Even high-quality scientific and technical information is of only limited value in EM decision-making if it is not understood and accepted by the Department of Energy's stakeholders. That is because the Department operates in a political environment in which citizen support is essential to obtain funding and, in many cases, to avoid costly and protracted litigation or similar consequences. Moreover, the Department's openness policy and requirements by many environmental laws compel the Department to make the information on which its decisions are based available for public scrutiny.

In many instances, the Department has failed to communicate the scientific and technical basis of important decisions. An example is a 1991 decision to build an incinerator at the Savannah River Site in South Carolina. The public documents initially prepared for the facility used outdated information on waste generation at the site and did not thoroughly discuss issues associated with the incineration of off-site waste. Both those failings attracted public concern and had to be re-addressed by the Department.

The reasons for the Department's lack of successful communication are varied. In some instances, the Department did not internally understand the project and so was unable to explain the rationale clearly. In others, the Department had the technical information but lacked the communication channels to work effectively with the public.

In other cases, however, the Department has been more successful—often with substantial assistance from skilled, independent facilitators or technical experts. A frequently praised example is the evaluation of land-use options at the Fernald Site in Ohio. Citizens reviewed levels of contamination, remediation alternatives, and other factors and came to agreement with the Department about remediation goals. Another example is the storage of special nuclear materials at the Rocky Flats Environmental Technology Site in Colorado; the Department at first assumed that citizens would object to a new facility but, after describing the technical issues, discovered that citizens were open to the idea.

Recommendations:

1. The Department of Energy should improve its own abilities, and those of its contractors, to communicate scientific and technical information. The various community-relations personnel in the Department system, as well as program and project managers, need the tools to communicate effectively with a variety of audiences and their understanding of program-wide and complex-wide issues needs to be sufficient to ensure that they can discuss matters beyond their immediate concern or expertise.

2. The Department of Energy should also make better use of outside resources in communicating scientific and technical information. That can include working with independent professionals. Another component of the effort can be providing funds to concerned community groups so that they can develop their own technical understanding and expertise. Indeed, the Department has already provided some such grants. It should, however, further define the selection and performance criteria for the awards. The experience of other federal agencies might be helpful in this regard.

Issue: It is important to meld public concerns and scientific and technical information into decision-making.

Many of the decisions faced by the EM Program cannot be made strictly within a box created by scientific and technical information. Practical factors compel consideration of cost and other resource limitations (including sometimes those of regulatory agencies). Political factors that influence decisions include socioeconomic impacts, cultural demands, such policy issues as nonproliferation, and public concerns.

A decision that is not supported by sound scientific and technical understanding might not succeed or might result in unnecessary costs or risks. The challenge for EM managers is to bring together a variety of factors into a well-balanced, implementable decision. That is inherently a dynamic process in which the elements of individual decisions will vary with the nature of the activity (which can range from groundwater remediation to nuclear-material stabilization) and with local concerns.

Recommendation:

The Department of Energy should seek to improve understanding and communication of the role of scientific and technical information relative to other factors in its decision-making. It should identify the role of public participation in the decision-making process. To be useful, public participation should be designed to address well-defined issues, occur early enough to influence outcomes, and have clear mechanisms for considering and responding to public comments.

References

Alternative Futures for the Department of Energy National Laboratories, prepared by the Secretary of Energy Advisory Board. February 1995. The report, also know as the Galvin Task Force, examines the role of Department of Energy National Laboratories and reviews the Department of Energy Environmental Management Program. Strongly critical of its activities, the report recommends changes in governance, economic role, science and engineering role, and environmental role. One of the most important challenges facing the Department and its laboratories to achieve greater integration of its various applied and fundamental energy R&D programs. Many fields of research and technology development could make up an appropriate energy agenda for the laboratories.

Benchmarking for Change: A Workshop Resulting from the RI/FS Benchmarking Study, February 1995. Organized by the Department of Energy Office of Environmental Restoration. The workshop summaries are not yet available, but copies of the presentations have been compiled. The workshop, chaired by Ned Larson (EM-45) focused on the highlights of the Remedial Investigation/Feasibility Study (RI/FS) Benchmarking study. Such issues as partnerships, project management, procurement, and pilot projects were discussed in breakout sessions.

Building Consensus Through Risk Assessment and Risk Management in the Department of Energy Environmental Remediation Program, NRC (National Research Council). 1994a. National Academy Press, Washington, D.C.

Cleaning Up the Department of Energy's Nuclear Weapons Complex, Congress of the United States, Congressional Budget Office, May 1994. The report outlines the Department's environmental goals and its cleanup program, including such policy issues as understanding risks, weighing costs and benefits, setting priorities, and investing in the development of technologies. The report acknowledges that the Department's cleanup program must address a problem that was created and largely ignored over the last 50 years. The department is faced with doing so during an especially tight budget climate. CBO recommends that understanding of risks and costs better would be the best way to determine priorities for allocating the scarce cleanup funds. It also recommends investing more heavily in technology development, delaying technically difficult projects, and cutting overhead costs to improve the efficiency of cleanup efforts. In addition, new management systems might help the Department of Energy and Congress track the performance of cleanup projects.

Complex Cleanup: The Environmental Legacy of Nuclear Weapons Production, OTA (U.S. Congress, Office of Technology Assessment), 1991. OTA-O484. U.S. Government Printing Office, Washington, D.C.

Environmental Management 1995: Progress and Plans of the Environmental Management Program, February 1995, US Department of Energy, Office of Environmental Management. The report identifies 1994 accomplishments in the topics established as goals of the Environmental Management Program:

- Eliminate and manage urgent risks in the system.
- Emphasize health and safety of workers and the public.
- Establish a system that is managerially and financially in control.
- Demonstrate tangible results.
- Focus technology development on overcoming obstacles to progress.
- Establish a stronger partnership between the Department and its stakeholders.

National programs and site summaries provide an overview of the activities in environmental regulation, waste management, environmental restoration, technology development, nuclear-material and -facilities stabilization, safety and health, risk management and priority-setting, and public accountability and outreach.

Hanford Integrated Planning Process: 1993 Hanford Site Specific Science and Technology Plan. Pacific Northwest Laboratory. 1993. U.S. Department of Energy Richland Operations Office Report DOE/RL-93-38. Richland, WA.

Health and Ecological Risks at the US Department of Energy's Nuclear Weapons Complex: A Qualitative Evaluation. Consortium for Environment Risk Evaluation (A Tulane/Xavier Program for the US Department of Energy). CERE Interim Risk Report. March 1995.

Independent Technical Review of the Brookhaven National Laboratory Environmental Restoration Program. June 1995. US Department of Energy, Chicago Operations Office, chartered an Independent technical review team to assess the Brookhaven National Laboratory (BNL) Environmental Restoration Program on the basis of commercial business practices and metrics and to recommend improvements if commercial and BNL practices, processes, or performance differed substantially. The overriding environmental-restoration goal in the commercial realm was defined to protect human health and the environment within the legal framework and within costs and schedules while providing immediate, open communication with interested and affected parties. In industry, protecting the ability to make money was considered paramount, so liability was often reduced quickly by investments in environmental activities. The team provided recommendations for business-process improvements and commercial environmental-restoration strategies.

Independent Technical Review of Environmental Restoration at Los Alamos National Laboratory, January 1995. Conducted by the Environmental Management Program at the Los Alamos National Laboratory. "To assess the barriers facing the program and develop approaches to ensure restoration success," the independent technical review team developed commercial standards by which to compare the restoration activities at Los Alamos. Benchmarking analysis included costs of operation.

Independent Technical Review of the Rocky Flats Program, June 1995. US Department of Energy, Office of Nuclear Material and Facility Stabilization, requested an independent technical review of the FY 1995 liability reduction and building baseline activities at the Rocky Flats Environmental Technology Site. To achieve liability reduction and improve efficiency, it was recommended that the DOE Rocky Flats Field Office senior management translate the strategic plan into a work logic based on budget and contractor performance measures. The change from a manage and operate (M&O) contractor to a performance based integrating contractor (PBIC) was thought to provide a unique opportunity to establish a new working relationship based on commercial business-like conduct and cleanup.

Management Changes Needed to Expand Use of Innovative Cleanup Technologies, US General Accounting Office, August 1994. The report identifies internal and external barriers to the use of new environmental technologies. It notes that although the Department has spent much to develop waste-cleanup technologies, little new technology is being implemented in the agency's cleanup actions. Part of the agency's problem, the report notes, is that the Department does not have a well-coordinated and fully integrated technology-development program. The Department's plan to restructure its technology-development programs is a step toward alleviating the problem. Field offices will also consider new and innovative technologies more seriously.

Organization and Staffing Review, January 1994. Office of Assistant Secretary for Environmental Restoration and Waste Management. At the request of the Assistant Secretary of Environmental Restoration and Waste Management, the Office of the Assistant Secretary for Human Resources and Administration led a review of program-related organizations, their staffing, and the associated environmental-management functions at headquarters and field locations. The review provides a perspective on how environmental-management programs are being administered by federal personnel and what issues attended their performance.

Project Performance Metrics Study, November 1993. Prepared by Independent Project Analysis, Inc., Reston, Virginia. The report was commissioned by the Office of Environmental Restoration and Waste Management (EM) of the US Department of Energy to asses the status of the EM project systems and to provide a baseline for measuring improvements against industry and other organizations. The report compares key measures of the environmental restoration and waste management project systems with the Independent Project Analysis proprietary industry Environmental Remediation and Capital Projects databases. The study establishes a comparison with industry and other organizations with respect to cost, schedule performance, project duration, and management turnover. Conclusions are drawn about the competitiveness of the project systems, and recommendations identify opportunities for improvement.

Ranking Hazardous-Waste Sites for Remedial Action, NRC (National Research Council). 1994b. National Academy Press, Washington, D.C.

Report of the Defense Science Board Task Force on Environmental Security, Department of Defense, Office of the Undersecretary of Defense, Acquisition and Technology, April 1995. The DOD environmental-remediation effort is a multi-billion-dollar endeavor. Among the possibilities for improvement that the report addresses is acceleration of environmental-technology development and deployment. It notes that many existing technologies offer substantial potential for risk or cost reduction that is not being realized, in part because of regulatory barriers. It identifies the barriers to deployment of new environmental technology as the worst bottleneck and expresses concern that with today's shrinking environmental budgets sufficient environmental science and technology investments that could reduce future costs will not be made. The group made several recommendations for accelerating technology development and deployment, including devoting an additional $150 million/year for accelerated environmental-technology demonstration and verification, clarifying assignment of responsibility, developing a set of incentives for federal site directors to use new technologies, and expanding cooperation among agencies and with industry.

Risks and the Risk Debate: Searching for Common Ground, The First Steps, June 1995. US Department of Energy, Office of Environmental Management. The Department has taken preliminary steps in the creation of a department-wide uniform process to evaluate risks to the environment and to health. Ultimately, this process should be capable of identifying the location and situations that pose the most serious risks across the nation to workers, the public, and the environment. Imminent risks to the environment and health should be of highest priority for action. For non-imminent risks, risk assessment should be used to identify the benefits of risk reduction as part of overall cost-benefit analyses, which should form the basis for further priority-setting and the timely resolution of contamination problems that must be addressed as required by law or compliance agreements.

Technology Needs Crosswalk Report, First Edition, Abridged Version, Chem-Nuclear Geotech, Inc. 1993. U.S. Department of Energy Albuquerque Field Office Report DOE/ID/12584-117 Ed. 1, Grand Junction, CO.

Train Wreck Along the River of Money—An Evaluation of the Hanford Cleanup, 1994. Written at the request of the US Senate Committee on Energy and Natural Resources, the report evaluates the cleanup of the Hanford Nuclear Reservation in Washington state. It critically examines such issues as cost of cleanup, management of programs, regulatory compliance, assignment of responsibilities, and future land use.

Appendix A
Charge to the Committee

U.S. Department of Energy
Washington, DC 20585

January 11, 1995
[Receipt]

Dr. Bruce Alberts
President, National Academy of Sciences
2101 Constitution Avenue, NW
Washington, DC 20418

Dear Dr. Alberts:

The National Academy of Sciences has a proven track record in providing the Department of Energy with scientific analyses critical to the success of the Environmental Management program. Faced with constrained budgets and the need to develop a system that works better and costs less, the Department once again would be aided by an analysis by the Academy. It is recognized that the cleanup problems now facing the Department and the Nation require a total re-engineering of existing systems and a thorough examination of the scientific, engineering, and institutional barriers to achieving a more cost-effective stewardship of the Nation's resources. This examination should be far more comprehensive than past analyses, which have involved subject experts in narrow fields.

Given the enormity of the Environmental Management Program, it is envisioned that a comprehensive evaluation will be more successful if it is focused around a few broad areas of major concern. Suggested topics include priority setting, timing and staging of activities, technology development, management and organizational systems, and regulatory measures.

Discussion on these and other issues would start with a series of public fora, which would then lead to an intense summer study. The public fora would provide options and observations for the summer study, while allowing for educational exchanges between stakeholders, scientists and decision makers. The summer study, attended by nationally recognized experts, would help frame options and factors for decision making. I would like to see the results of the study by December 1, 1995.

I have asked Admiral Richard Guimond and Dr. Carol Henry to be the principal Department points of contact for framing the specific questions and context in which the Academy reviewers would perform their analysis. This work will be performed under cooperative agreement #DE-AC01-94EW54069. I look forward to working with the Academy to obtain the scientific and engineering community's views on these very important issues.

Sincerely,

Thomas P. Grumbly
Assistant Secretary for
Environmental Management

Enclosure

PROPOSED NATIONAL ACADEMY OF SCIENCE FORA

The five proposed fora topics encompass major issues that the Environmental Management program is likely to encounter in the next several years. The Department will work with the Academy to further define the content and range of issues to be evaluated within each fora.

Priority Setting

The Priority Setting forum will examine the process of prioritizing Environmental Management activities, and how the process incorporates societal values, costs, current regulations, and risks to the environment, public health, and worker safety.

Timing and Staging of Activities

The Timing and Staging forum will examine how the Environmental Management program can schedule technology development and remediation/restoration efforts such that cost savings are maximized and risks to the environment, public, and workers are minimized.

Technology

The Technology forum will examine all aspects of how technology can best be developed and utilized to aid the federal remediation process.

Management and Organizational Systems

The Management and Organizational Systems forum will examine the management and organizational systems which are most likely to achieve Environmental Management program goals.

Regulatory Measures

The Regulatory Measures forum will examine how the performance of the Environmental Management program could be improved through regulatory measures such as new statues, revised statues, and revised regulatory agreements.

Appendix B
Workshop Agendas

NATIONAL RESEARCH COUNCIL

COMMITTEE TO EVALUATE THE SCIENCE, ENGINEERING, AND HEALTH BASIS OF THE DOE'S ENVIRONMENTAL MANAGEMENT PROGRAM

Evaluation of Regulatory Measures Workshop

National Academy of Sciences Building
2101 Constitution Avenue, NW
Washington, DC 20418

June 19–20, 1995

AGENDA

Monday, June 19

Workshop—Plenary Session—Auditorium

4:00 pm   Welcome
E. William Colglazier, Executive Officer, National Research Council
Don Clay, Workshop Chair

4:10   **Carol J. Henry**, Science and Policy Director, Office of Integrated Risk Management, Department of Energy (DOE)

Ellen Livingston-Behan, Acting Executive Officer, Office of Environmental Management, Department of Energy (DOE)

4:50   Question and Answer

5:30   Recess

Tuesday, June 20

Workshop—Plenary Session—Auditorium

9:00 am   Welcome
Don Clay, Workshop Chair

169

Panel 1: Views from Office of Environment, Safety, and Health of Department of Energy

9:10   **Andrew Lawrence**, Director, Compliance Assessment Division, Office of Environmental Policy and Assistance, DOE/ESH

9:25   **Joseph Fitzgerald, Jr.**, Deputy Assistant Secretary for Worker Health and Safety, Office of Environment, Safety and Health, Department of Energy

9:40   Questions & Answers; Issue Identification

Panel 2: Views from the Other Federal Agencies

9:50   **Elizabeth Cotsworth**, Deputy Director, Office of Solid Waste, Environmental Protection Agency

10:05   **Camilla Warren**, Chief of DOE Remedial Section, Federal Facilities Branch, Environmental Protection Agency, Region IV

10:20   **John Austin**, Chief, Performance Assessment and Hydrology Branch, Division of Waste Management, Nuclear Regulatory Commission

10:35   Questions & Answers; Issue Identification

10:45   Break—Great Hall

Panel 3: Views from DOE Sites and Outside of the Federal Government

11:00   **Sam Goodhope**, Special Assistant Attorney General, Office of the Attorney General, State of Texas

11:15   **Joseph Nagel**, Nagel Environmental Consulting (former Director, Department of Environmental Quality for the State of Idaho)

11:30   **Don Macdonald**, Executive Assistant to the Manager of the Idaho Operations Office, Department of Energy

11:45   **Louis Bogar**, Independent Consultant
            (former Vice-President, Westinghouse Materials Company of Ohio)

12:00 pm   **Adam Babich**, Editor-in-chief of *The Environmental Law Reporter*, Environmental Law Institute

12:15   Question & Answers; Issue Identification

12:30   Break

Board Room

Roundtable Discussion: committee, speakers, invited discussants

1:30   Overview
           Don Clay, Workshop Chair

Roundtable discussants (in addition to committee members and morning speakers):

Elmer Akin, Chief, Office of Health Assessment, Waste Management Division, Environmental Protection Agency, Region IV

Lokesh Chaturvedi, Deputy Director, Environmental Evaluation Group of the New Mexico Institute of Mining and Technology

Tom Isaacs, Executive Director, Advisory Committee on External Regulation of Department of Energy Nuclear Safety

David O'Very, Attorney Advisor/Special Assistant to the Director, Office of Radiation and Indoor Air

Suzanne Rudzinski, Director of the Office of Policy Analysis, Office of Environmental Management, Department of Energy

Milton Russell, Director, Joint Institute for Energy and Environment, Professor of Economics, University of Tennessee

4:25   Closing: **Don Clay**

4:30   Workshop ends

NATIONAL RESEARCH COUNCIL

COMMITTEE TO EVALUATE THE SCIENCE, ENGINEERING, AND HEALTH BASIS OF THE DOE'S ENVIRONMENTAL MANAGEMENT PROGRAM

Priority Setting, Timing & Staging of Environmental Management Activities Workshop

National Academy of Sciences Building
2101 Constitution Avenue, NW
Washington, DC 20418

June 26–27, 1995

AGENDA

Monday, June 26

Lecture Room

Workshop—Plenary Session

4:00 pm	Welcome
	E. William Colglazier, Executive Officer, National Research Council
	Toby Clark, Committee Chair
	Executive Director, Clean Sites, Inc.
4:10	**Carol J. Henry**, Science and Policy Director, Office of Integrated Risk Management, Department of Energy (DOE)
4:50	Questions & Answers
5:30	Recess

Tuesday, June 27

Lecture Room

Workshop—Plenary Session

9:00 am	Welcome: **Toby Clark**, Committee Chair
9:15	**Panel 1: View from the Field**

Douglas L. Weaver, Independent Review Program Manager, Sandia National Laboratories

Bob Anderson, Project Leader, Prioritization, Environmental Health and Safety Division, Los Alamos National Laboratory

Curtis Travis, Director, Center for Risk Management, Oak Ridge National Laboratory

10:15   Questions & Answers; Issue Identification

10:45   Break

11:00   **Panel 2: View from the Outside**

John Applegate, Professor, College of Law, University of Cincinnati; and Chair, Fernald Citizens Task Force

Susan Wiltshire, Vice President, JK Research Associates

Toby Michelena, Coordinator of Tank Waste Remediation Systems, Nuclear Waste Program, Washington State Department of Ecology

Lee Merkhofer, Principal, Applied Decision Analysis, Inc.

12:00 pm   Questions & Answers; Issue Identification

12:30   Break

Lecture Room

Roundtable Discussion: committee, speakers, invited discussants

1:30   Overview: **Toby Clark**, Committee Chair

Roundtable discussants (in addition to committee members and morning speakers)

Brian Costner, Director, Energy Research Foundation

Julie D'Ambrosia, Program Manager, EcoTech Associates, Inc.

Robert N. Ferguson, Oversight Administrator, Idaho National Engineering Laboratory, State of Idaho

Mark Gilbertson, Program Director, Office of Integrated Risk Management, Department of Energy (DOE)

4:25   Closing: **Toby Clark**, Committee Chair

4:30   Workshop ends

NATIONAL RESEARCH COUNCIL

COMMITTEE TO EVALUATE THE
SCIENCE, ENGINEERING, AND HEALTH BASIS
OF THE DOE'S ENVIRONMENTAL MANAGEMENT PROGRAM

Workshop on Utilization of Science, Engineering, and Technology in the Environmental Management Program

National Academy of Sciences Building
2101 Constitution Avenue, NW
Washington, DC 20418

July 11–14, 1995

AGENDA

Tuesday, July 11

Workshop—Plenary Session Auditorium

4:00 pm   Welcome
E. William Colglazier, Executive Officer, National Research Council
Frank Parker, Workshop Chair

4:10   **Carol Henry & Mac Lankford**, Department of Energy (DOE)

4:50   Question and answer

5:30   Adjourn to **Auditorium Gallery** for reception

Wednesday, July 12

Workshop—Plenary Session—Lecture Room

9:00 am   Welcome
Frank Parker, Workshop Chair

Presentations: Views from the DOE

9:15   **Mac Lankford & Teresa Fryberger**, Department of Energy (DOE)

9:40   **Harry Harmon**, Savannah River

10:05   Questions & answers; Issue identification

10:20   Break—Lecture Room

              Presentations: View from the Outside

10:30   **Walter Kovalick**, EPA

10:50   **John Carberry**, DuPont

11:20   **Robert Hightower**, Lockheed Martin Energy Systems

11:40   **Rebecca T. Parkin**, Public Health Considerations in Environmental Cleanup

12:00 pm   Question & answers; Issue identification

Workshop—Roundtable—Lecture Room

Roundtable Discussion: committee, workshop participants, and speakers

1:30   Overview: **Frank Parker**, Workshop Chair

              Roundtable discussion leaders:

              Teresa Fryberger, DOE

              Gretchen H. McCabe, Battelle

              Pat Whitfield, Environmental Management Consulting

              Christopher Nagel, Molten Metal Technology

              David Rubenson, Rand Corporation

              Toby Clark, Clean Sites

4:25   Closing: **Frank Parker**, Workshop Chair

4:30   Workshop ends

NATIONAL RESEARCH COUNCIL

COMMITTEE TO EVALUATE THE SCIENCE, ENGINEERING, AND HEALTH BASIS OF THE DOE'S ENVIRONMENTAL MANAGEMENT PROGRAM

Subcommittee on Integration of Science, Engineering, and Health in Program Implementation

National Academy of Sciences Building
2101 Constitution Avenue, NW
Washington, DC 20418

August 29–30, 1995

AGENDA

Tuesday, August 29

Lecture Room

Workshop—Plenary Session

4:00 pm   Welcome

E. William Colglazier, Executive Officer, National Research Council

Victoria Tschinkel, Workshop Chair
Senior Consultant, Landers and Parsons

4:10   **Rear Admiral Richard J. Guimond**, Principal Deputy Assistant Secretary for Environmental Management, Department of Energy

4:50   Questions & Answers

5:30   Adjourn for day

Wednesday, August 30

Lecture Room

Workshop—Plenary Session

8:30 am   Welcome; **Victoria Tschinkel**, Workshop Chair

Panel 1: View from DOE Headquarters

Moderator: **Victoria Tschinkel**

8:35   **Gail Pesyna**, Deputy Assistant Secretary for Management and Finance, Office of Environmental Management, Department of Energy

8:55   **Ken Glozer**, Senior Advisor to the Assistant Secretary for Environmental Management, Department of Energy

9:15   Questions & Answers; Issue Identification

Panel 2: View from the DOE Sites

Moderator: **Brian Costner**, committee member

9:35   **Hank McGuire**, Vice President of Business Development, Scientific Ecology Group, Westinghouse Corporation

9:50   **Philip Thullen,** Program Manager, Independent Technical Review, Environmental Management Program, Red Team Reviews

10:05   **John Applegate**, Chair, Fernald Citizens Task Force

10:20   Questions & Answers; Issue Identification

10:40   Break

Panel 3: Perspectives Outside of DOE

Moderator: **Maxine Savitz**, committee member

10:55   **Philip Palmer**, Senior Environmental Fellow, Dupont Specialty Chemicals Corporate Remediation, E.I. du Pont de Nemours & Company

11:10   **Dan Abramowicz**, Manager, Environmental Laboratory, General Electric Corporate Research and Development

         Kevin Holtzclaw, Senior Program Manager, Environmental Remediation Program, General Electric Company

11:30   **Patricia Rivers**, Assistant Deputy Under Secretary of Defense for Environmental Cleanup, Department of Defense

11:45   **Richard Marty**, Senior Engineer Specialist, Jason Associates Corporation

12:00   Questions & Answers; Issue Identification

12:30   Lunch

Lecture Room

1:30 pm   Overview: **Victoria Tschinkel**, Workshop Chair

         Roundtable Discussion: committee, speakers, discussants

         Roundtable Discussants: (*in addition to committee and speakers*)

         Doug Weaver, Program Manager, Independent Technical Review

         Deborah Bennett, Staff Member, Environmental Management Program, Red Team Reviews

4:25   Closing: **Victoria Tschinkel**, Workshop Chair

4:30   Workshop ends

Appendix C
Biographical Information on Committee Members

BIOGRAPHICAL INFORMATION FOR MEMBERS OF THE
SYNTHESIS SUBCOMMITTEE

John F. Ahearne is the Executive Director of Sigma Xi, the Scientific Research Society; Lecturer in Public Policy, Duke University; and Adjunct Scholar, Resources for the Future. He has served as Vice President and Senior Fellow for Resources for the Future; Commissioner and Chairman of the U.S. Nuclear Regulatory Commission; System Analyst for the White House Energy Office; Deputy Assistant Secretary of Energy; and Deputy and Deputy Assistant Secretary of Defense. He received his MS from Cornell University and his MA and PhD from Princeton University.

Andrew P. Caputo is an Attorney with the Natural Resources Defense Council's Nuclear Program. He was previously Associate Attorney and then Project Attorney with the Sierra Club Legal Defense Fund from 1990–93. He received his A.B. in history from Brown University and holds a JD from Yale Law School.

Edwin H. Clark II is President of Clean Sites, Inc., in Alexandria, VA. He is former Secretary of the Delaware Department of Natural Resources and Environmental Control, Vice President of the Conservation Foundation, and Acting Assistant Administrator of the pesticides and toxic substances program in the Environmental Protection Agency. He holds a PhD in applied economics from Princeton University.

Don Clay is President of Don Clay Associates, a public policy consulting firm devoted to solid and hazardous waste issues. From 1989–93 he headed the EPA's Office of Solid Waste and Emergency Response where he implemented many reforms including the Superfund Revitalization Initiative and Accelerated Cleanup Model. Prior to this position, he was Deputy Assistant Administrator of the Office of Air and Radiation, 1986–89; and Director of the Office of Toxic Substances, 1981–86 at the EPA. He holds an MS from Ohio State University.

Douglas M. Costle is Chairman and Distinguished Fellow at the Institute for Sustainable Communities based in Montpelier, Vermont. He is former Administrator of the US EPA, appointed by President Jimmy Carter in 1976 and served until 1981. Mr. Costle is a former Fellow at the Smithsonian's Woodrow Wilson International Center for Scholars; Visiting Scholar at Harvard's School of Public Health; and Adjunct Lecturer at Harvard's John F. Kennedy School of Government. He was Dean of Vermont Law School from 1987–91 and greatly strengthened the program under his tenure. In November 1992, Mr. Costle was appointed to lead the Clinton Transition Team on Energy. He holds a JD from Chicago Law School.

James R. Curtiss is a Partner in the law firm of Winston and Strawn in Washington, DC. He was previously Commissioner of the Nuclear Regulatory Commission, 1988–93. He also served as Associate Counsel for the Senate Committee on Environment and Public Works for the U.S. Senate from 1981–88. From 1979–81, Mr. Curtiss was Staff Attorney in the Regulations Division for the Office of the Executive Legal Director at the Nuclear Regulatory Commission. Mr. Curtiss holds a JD from the University of Nebraska.

Frank L. Parker is Distinguished Professor of Environmental and Water Resources Engineering at Vanderbilt University. Dr. Parker served as Chairman of the Board of Radioactive Waste Management of NAS/NRC and is a member of several environmental advisory committees including the Environmental Management Advisory Board of the Department of Energy. He is a member of the National Academy of Engineering. He received his BS from the Massachusetts Institute of Technology and his PhD in civil engineering from Harvard University.

Victoria J. Tschinkel is Senior Consultant for environmental issues at the law firm of Landers and Parsons in Tallahassee, Florida. From 1981 to 1987, she was Secretary of the Florida Department of Environmental Regulation, serving as the agency's chief administrative and policy officer. Ms. Tschinkel is Chairman of the Advisory Council of the Gas Research Institute and a Fellow of the National Academy of Public Administration. She received her B.S in zoology from the University of California at Berkeley.

John T. Whetten is a Senior Applications Consultant to Motorola in Los Alamos, NM. He was previously Associate Director for Energy and Technology at Los Alamos National Laboratory. Dr. Whetten has many years of experience in research for the U.S. Geological Survey in Seattle; and in university teaching, research and administration at the University of Washington. He holds a PhD in geology from Princeton University.

BIOGRAPHICAL INFORMATION FOR MEMBERS
OF THE SUBCOMMITTEE ON THE EVALUATION
OF REGULATORY MEASURES

Don Clay is President of Don Clay Associates, a public policy consulting firm devoted to solid and hazardous waste issues. From 1989–93 he headed the EPA's Office of Solid Waste and Emergency Response where he implemented many reforms including the Superfund Revitalization Initiative and Accelerated Cleanup Model. Prior to this position, he was Deputy Assistant Administrator of the Office of Air and Radiation, 1986–89; and Director of the Office of Toxic Substances, 1981–86 at the EPA. He holds an MS from Ohio State University.

Andrew P. Caputo is an Attorney with the Natural Resources Defense Council's Nuclear Program. He was previously Associate Attorney and then Project Attorney with the Sierra Club Legal Defense Fund from 1990–93. He received his A.B. in history from Brown University and holds a JD from Yale Law School.

James R. Curtiss is a Partner in the law firm of Winston and Strawn in Washington, DC. He was previously Commissioner of the Nuclear Regulatory Commission, 1988–93. He also served as Associate Counsel for the Senate Committee on Environment and Public Works for the U.S. Senate from 1981–88. From 1979–81, Mr. Curtiss was Staff Attorney in the Regulations Division for the Office of the Executive Legal Director at the Nuclear Regulatory Commission. Mr. Curtiss holds a JD from the University of Nebraska.

Marshall E. Drummond is President of Eastern Washington University. He has chaired several public advisory groups, including the Hanford Tank Waste Task Force and the Hanford Future Site Use Working Group. He received a doctor of education degree from the University of San Francisco.

Daniel S. Miller is First Assistant Attorney General with the Colorado Department of Law in Denver where he supervises the hazardous-waste and solid-waste unit, representing it on all RCRA, CERCLA, and solid-waste matters. He has expertise in environmental compliance at federal facilities, including Rocky Flats and Rocky Mountain Arsenal. He holds a JD from the University of California, Berkeley.

Bernard J. Reilly is Corporate Counsel for DuPont Legal in the Environment Group where he is responsible for plant permit and compliance issues, corrective actions, and Superfund sites in New Jersey. He is also responsible for the overall management of DuPont's legal involvement in Superfund and its reauthorization. Mr. Reilly holds a BS in engineering from the United States Marine Academy, an MS in mechanical engineering from Brown University, and a JD from the University of Virginia.

Mary Riveland is the Director of the Washington State Department of Ecology, the state's primary environmental agency. Ms. Riveland is also a member of the Environmental Management Advisory Board and the Governor's Task Force on Regulatory Reform, and serves on the executive board of the Environmental Council of the States. She holds a BA in political science from the University of Washington.

BIOGRAPHICAL INFORMATION FOR MEMBERS OF THE SUBCOMMITTEE ON PRIORITY SETTING, TIMING AND STAGING

Edwin H. Clark II is President of Clean Sites, Inc., in Alexandria, VA. He is former Secretary of the Delaware Department of Natural Resources and Environmental Control, Vice President of the Conservation Foundation, and Acting Assistant Administrator of the pesticides and toxic substances program in the Environmental Protection Agency. He holds a PhD in applied economics from Princeton University.

Hugh J. Campbell Jr. is Environmental Manager at DuPont with over 20 years of experience in the environmental field consulting on and managing water, wastewater, solid/hazardous waste, geological engineering, site investigation and remedial action issues. From 1972–87 he did consulting work relating to industrial waste management/control for E.I. du Pont de Nemours and Company. Dr. Campbell holds an MS in sanitary engineering from the University of Maine at Orono, and a PhD in environmental engineering from Purdue University.

Mary R. English is Associate Director of the Energy, Environment, and Resources Center at the University of Tennessee, and a Senior Fellow at its Waste Management and Education Institute. She previously worked in environmental planning for state government and as a consultant. She holds an MS in regional planning from the University of Massachusetts and a PhD in Sociology from the University of Tennessee.

Donald R. Gibson Jr. is Department Manager of the Systems Analysis Department and Acting Lab Manager at TRW's Ballistic Missiles Division in its survivability and engineering laboratory. Prior to these positions he was a design physicist and senior project engineer. Dr. Gibson holds an MS and PhD in nuclear engineering from the University of Illinois.

Robert E. Hazen is Chief of the Bureau of Risk Assessment at the New Jersey Department of Environmental Protection since 1984. He is formerly an Assistant Professor in the Environmental Health Science Program at Hunter College, City University of New York. Dr. Hazen holds an MS from Fairleigh Dickinson University and a PhD in biology and environmental health from New York University.

Thomas Leschine is Associate Professor in the School of Marine Affairs at the University of Washington. He is a former Fellow in Marine Policy and a Policy Associate at the Woods Hole Oceanographic Institute. His major research interest is in the area of environmental decision making as it relates to marine pollution control. Dr. Leschine holds a PhD from the University of Pittsburgh.

Robert H. Neill is Director of the Environmental Evaluation Group in Albuquerque, NM. EEG performs independent evaluations of the health and environmental impacts of the Waste Isolation Pilot Plant, a DOE repository for the disposal of defense transuranic wastes. He was previously a Commissioned Officer in the Bureau of Radiological Health, US Public Health Service for 23 years. Mr. Neill holds an ME from Stevens Institute of Technology and an MS in radiation hygiene from Harvard University.

Lynne M. Preslo is Senior Vice President for Technical Programs at Earth Tech in Berkeley, CA. She is a hydrogeologist and California Registered Geologist with more than 15 years of environmental consulting experience. Ms. Preslo holds a BS in applied earth sciences and an MS in hydrogeology from Stanford University.

Anne E. Smith is Principal and Vice President at Decision Focus, Inc. in Washington, DC. Prior to her current position she has been an independent consultant, an EPA consultant, and an EPA economist. Dr. Smith holds an MA and a PhD in economics, with PhD minor in engineering-economic systems, from Stanford University.

Mervyn L. Tano is General Counsel and Senior Environmental Programs Manager for the Council of Energy Resources Tribes based in Denver, CO. He advises and assists tribes on high-level radioactive-waste issues; legal, administrative, and technical system requirements; and environmental, health, and safety implications. He also advises the DOE and nuclear-negotiation officials on tribal jurisdictional issues related to high-level waste management and transportation. Mr. Tano holds a JD from Brigham Young University.

BIOGRAPHICAL INFORMATION FOR MEMBERS OF THE SUBCOMMITTEE ON UTILIZATION OF SCIENCE, ENGINEERING, AND TECHNOLOGY

Frank L. Parker is Distinguished Professor of Environmental and Water Resources Engineering at Vanderbilt University. Dr. Parker served as Chairman of the Board of Radioactive Waste Management of NAS/NRC and is a member of several environmental advisory committees including the Environmental Management Advisory Board of the Department of Energy. He is a member of the National Academy of Engineering. He received his BS from the Massachusetts Institute of Technology and his PhD in civil engineering from Harvard University.

John F. Ahearne is the Executive Director of Sigma Xi, the Scientific Research Society, and Adjunct Scholar, Resources for the Future. He has served as Vice President and Senior Fellow for Resources for the Future; Commissioner and Chairman of the U.S. Nuclear Regulatory Commission; System Analyst for the White House Energy Office; Deputy Assistant Secretary of Energy; and Deputy and Deputy Assistant Secretary of Defense. He received his MS from Cornell University and his MA and PhD from Princeton University.

Charles B. Andrews is President of S. S. Papadopulos & Associates, and directs projects involving quantitative ground water hydrology. He previously served as senior project hydrologist with Woodward-Clyde Consultants, where he worked on projects that included managing cleanup of Superfund sites. Dr. Andrews holds a PhD in geology from the University of Wisconsin.

Edgar Berkey is President and Co-Founder of the Center for Hazardous Materials Research, and the National Environmental Technology Applications Center, two non-profit environmental organizations in Pittsburgh, PA. Previously, he was founder and President of SynCo Consultants, Inc.; Vice President of Energy Impact Associates, and Manager and Senior Scientist at Westinghouse Research Laboratories. Dr. Berkey holds a PhD in engineering physics from Cornell University, and completed the Executive MBA Program at the University of Pittsburgh.

Harold K. Forsen is Foreign Secretary of the National Academy of Engineering. He is retired Senior Vice President and Director of Bechtel Hanford, Inc. He has been a consultant to many organizations including General Atomics, Oak Ridge and Argonne National Laboratories, Lawrence Radiation Laboratory, and Battelle Memorial Institute. Dr. Forsen is a member of the National Academy of Engineering and is on several advisory committees to DOE laboratories. He holds a PhD in electrical engineering from the University of California at Berkeley.

Walter Kovalick is the Director of the Technology Innovation Office, Office of Solid Waste and Emergency Response, United States Environmental Protection Agency. Prior to this position he served as Acting Deputy Administrator for the Office of Solid Waste and Emergency Response. For five years, until December 1989, he was the Deputy Director of the Superfund program. He holds an MBA from Harvard Business School and a PhD in public administration and policy from Virginia Polytechnic Institute.

Michael L. Mastracci is the Director of the Innovative Programs for TECHMATICS, Inc. of Fairfax, VA. From 1972–1995, he has held various positions in the Research office of the U.S. Environmental Protection Agency. Before working in government, he held a number of department level positions with the AMF and Wester Gear Corporations. He is an inventor, an international consultant and an active participant in a variety of industry and trade networks, and advisory commissions, all relating to environmental technology development.

Philip Palmer is a senior environmental fellow in the DuPont Chemicals Core Resources Section of the Corporate Remediation Group. He has over 15 years of experience in the field of remediation technology development. He currently heads a group of 40 that is evaluating remediation technologies. Palmer oversees development and pilot testing of new technologies on DuPont sites and assessment of the company's remediation technology needs. Mr. Palmer served as a leader and member of the Chemical Manufacturers Association RCRA Regulations Task Force from the inception of RCRA until 1990. He is a former CGER member. He hold a BS and an MS in chemical engineering from Cornell University. He holds an MS in environmental engineering from Drexel University.

Rebecca Tyrrell Parkin is concurrently the Director of Scientific, Professional and Section Affairs at the American Public Health Association and the President of Beccam Services where she specializes in occupational and environmental health, and policy analysis. Dr. Parkin was previously Assistant Commissioner in the Division of Occupational and Environmental Health, New Jersey Department of Health; Epidemiologist, Centers for Disease Control; and Chief of the Environmental Health Program, New Jersey Department of Health. She holds an MPH in environmental health and a PhD in epidemiology from Yale University.

Alfred Schneider is currently Emeritus Professor of Nuclear Engineering at Georgia Institute of Technology; and President of Schneider Labs Inc.

Prior to these positions Dr. Schneider was Director of Nuclear Technology of Allied General Nuclear Service in South Carolina. He is a member of the American Chemical Society, American Institute of Engineers, American Nuclear Society, and American Association for Advancement of Science. Dr. Schneider holds a PhD from the Polytechnic University of New York.

Christine Shoemaker is Professor and Chair of the Department of Environmental Engineering at Cornell University. Dr. Shoemaker has been a panel member for the NRC committee on pest control and the Environmental Studies Board's Scientific Council on Problems of the Environment. She was also a member of the FAO Expert Panel on Pest Management. Her research involves the application of optimization, statistical, and mathematical analysis to environmental problems. She holds a PhD in mathematics from the University of Southern California.

C. Herb Ward is Foyt Family Chair of Engineering, Professor of Environmental Science and Engineering and Ecology and Evolutionary Biology, and Director of the Energy and Environmental Systems Institute at Rice University. He has served on the National Research Council's Committee on Multimedia Approaches to Pollution Control, Advisory Committee on Multiagency Hazardous Wastes Research, and Committee on Alternatives for Ground Water Cleanup. Dr. Ward holds a PhD from Cornell University and an MPH from the University of Texas.

John T. Whetten is a Senior Applications Consultant to Motorola in Los Alamos, NM. He was previously Associate Director for Energy and Technology at Los Alamos National Laboratory. Dr. Whetten has many years of experience in research for the U.S. Geological Survey in Seattle; and in university teaching, research and administration at the University of Washington. He holds a PhD in geology from Princeton University.

Raymond G. Wymer is currently an independent consultant based in Oak Ridge, TN. Dr. Wymer is retired Director of the Chemical Technology Division at Oak Ridge National Laboratory where he worked for over 20 years. He also served as an Associate Professor at the Georgia Institute of Technology and as Chief Nuclear Chemist for Industrial Reactor Labs. Dr. Wymer holds a PhD from Vanderbilt University.

BIOGRAPHICAL INFORMATION FOR MEMBERS OF THE SUBCOMMITTEE ON THE INTEGRATION OF SCIENCE, ENGINEERING, AND HEALTH IN PROGRAM IMPLEMENTATION

Victoria J. Tschinkel is Senior Consultant for environmental issues at the law firm of Landers and Parsons in Tallahassee, Florida. From 1981 to 1987, she was Secretary of the Florida Department of Environmental Regulation, serving as the agency's chief administrative and policy officer. Ms. Tschinkel is Chairman of the Advisory Council of the Gas Research Institute and a Fellow of the National Academy of Public Administration. She received her B.S in zoology from the University of California at Berkeley.

Betsy Ancker-Johnson has been Chairman (pro bono) of the World Environment Center since 1988. She is retired Vice President of General Motors Corporation, Environmental Activities Staff, 1979–1992. She was Assistant Secretary of Science and Technology in the US Department of Commerce from 1973–77; and Associate Laboratory Director for Physical Research at National Laboratory in Argonne, IL, from 1977–79. She holds a PhD in physics from Tubingen University and several honorary degrees.

Philip Brodsky is Director of Corporate Research and Environmental Technology at Monsanto Company in St. Louis, Missouri. He first joined Monsanto as a senior research engineer in 1969 and has filled successive positions as research specialist, group leader, senior group leader, manager, and director of research and development before taking his current position in 1987. Dr. Brodsky holds a PhD in chemical engineering from Cornell University.

David S.C. Chu is currently Director of RAND's Washington Research Department. He is former Assistant Secretary of Defense for Program Analysis and Evaluation, US Department of Defense; Assistant Director, National Security and International Affairs Division, Congressional Budget Office; and Senior Economist and then Associate Head, Economics Department, Rand Corporation. Dr. Chu received his BA, MA, M. Phil., and PhD, all in economics, from Yale University.

Benjamin A. Cosgrove is retired Senior Vice President for Technical and Government Affairs for the Boeing Commercial Airplane Group and is a 44-year veteran employee. He was BCAG's senior executive on safety matters. In 1992 he became Senior VP for Technical and Government Affairs. Mr. Cosgrove is a member of the National Academy of Engineering. Mr. Cosgrove holds a BS from Notre Dame and an Honor Award from Notre Dame's College of Engineering.

Brian Costner has been Director of the Energy Research Foundation (ERF) in Columbia, SC, since June 1989. Mr. Costner was a member of the working group which established the charter for the SRS Citizens Advisory Board and is now a member of that Board and chair of the Board's subcommittee on Risk Management and future use. In September 1994, Mr. Costner was appointed to DOE's Environmental Management Advisory Board, where he serves on the Executive Committee, Risk Committee, Budget Committee, and as chair of the NEPA Compliance Practices Committee.

Robert C. Forney is retired Executive Vice President of E.I. du Pont de Nemours and Co. He joined Du Pont as Research Engineer in 1950 and advanced in various research, technical and marketing management positions. Mr. Forney is a member of the National Academy of Engineering, the Society of Chemical Industry, the American Chemical Society, the American Institute of Chemical Engineers, the American Association for the Advancement of Science and Sigma Xi. He holds an MS in industrial engineering and a PhD in chemical engineering from Purdue University.

James Johnson Jr., is Professor and Acting Dean of the School of Engineering at Howard University in Washington, DC. He is also a member of the Environmental Engineering Committee of US EPA's Science Advisory Board and of the National Research Council's Committee on the Remediation of Buried and Tank Wastes. Dr. Johnson is Associate Editor of the *Journal of Hazardous Materials*. He holds an MS from the University of Illinois and a PhD from the University of Delaware.

Mildred McClain is Executive Director of Citizens for Environmental Justice in Savannah, GA. She is also a Senior Consultant for Educational Enterprises providing advice to schools, organizations, businesses and national campaigns in the areas of organizational development, community development, grassroots organizing, crisis intervention, program planning, and many other areas. She is a former high school teacher and has directed community organizations on a variety of social issues. Dr. McClain received her doctorate of education from the Harvard Graduate School of Education.

Bernice K. McIntyre is President of B.K.McIntyre & Associates, Inc. She was previously Manager in the Utility Management Practice of Arthur D. Little, Inc.; and served as Chairman of the Massachusetts Department of Public Utilities prior to joining Arthur D. Little. Ms. McIntyre has extensive experience in telecommunications, utility and environmental regulation. She was a member of President Clinton and Vice President Gore's Transition Team to develop policy and personnel recommendations. She holds a JD from Boston University School of Law.

Maxine L. Savitz is currently General Manager of Ceramic Components at Allied Signal Aerospace Company. From 1979–83 she was Deputy Assistant Secretary for Conservation at the Department of Energy, followed by President of the Lighting Research Institute at the Department of Energy, 1983–85. Before joining her present company, Ms. Savitz was Assistant Vice President of Engineering at the Garrett Corporation. She is a member of the National Academy of Engineering and holds a PhD in organic chemistry from the Massachusetts Institute of Technology.

Appendix D
Biographical Information on Workshop Speakers and Participants

EVALUATION OF REGULATORY MEASURES WORKSHOP

Carol J. Henry is the Science and Policy Director of the Office of Integrated Risk Management at the Department of Energy (DOE). She is responsible for the development of major policies, systems and guidelines for DOE's Environmental Management risk management programs and activities and she reports directly to the Assistant Secretary for Environmental Management. From 1992–94 Dr. Henry was the Director of the Office of Environmental Health Hazard Assessment, California Environmental Protection Agency. She was previously the Executive Director of the International Life Sciences Institute's Risk Science Institute in Washington, DC. Dr. Henry holds a PhD in Microbiology from the University of Pittsburgh and has done post doctoral work at the Max Planck Institute in Tubingen, at Princeton University and at the Sloan Kettering Institute.

Ellen Livingston-Behan is Acting Executive Officer, Office of Environmental Management, Department of Energy (DOE).

Andrew Lawrence is Director of the Compliance Assistance Division, DOE. Prior to this he was Special Assistant to the Director of the Office of Environmental Compliance. Mr. Lawrence holds a BA in American Studies from Amherst College and an MS in Science and Technology Policy from American University.

Joseph Fitzgerald Jr. serves as the Deputy Assistant Secretary for Worker Health and Safety in the Department of Energy's Office of Environment, Safety, and Health. Prior to this position, he served as the Director of the Performance Assessment Division of the Department of Energy's Office of Nuclear Safety. In addition, he also served as the Department of Energy's Director of Safety Policy within the Office of the Assistant Secretary for Nuclear Safety. Mr. Fitzgerald holds a BS in Environmental Engineering and an MS in Public Health and Environmental Engineering from Tufts University and an MPH in Radiological Health Protection from the University of Minnesota.

Elizabeth Cotsworth is currently the Deputy Director of the EPA Office of Solid Waste. She has held a series of positions within the Office of Solid Waste since joining OSW in 1978. Most recently, Ms. Cotsworth was the Deputy Director, OSW Waste Management Division, where she was involved in implementing the RCRA land disposal restrictions program, performing national waste management capacity analysis, and developing hazardous waste combustion regulations. She holds a BA from Chatham College and an MA from the University of Virginia.

Camilla Warren is Chief of the DOE Remedial Section, Federal Facilities Branch, U.S. EPA Region IV. Prior to this she worked with the RCRA Compliance Unit also in Region IV. Ms. Warren has twelve years combined experience working on issues involving Superfund and RCRA. Her experience includes settlement negotiations involving Superfund sites and federal facility agreements with DOE. Ms. Warren holds a BS in Forest Hydrology from the University of Georgia and MS in Environmental Engineering from Clemson University.

John Austin is Chief of the Performance Assessment and Hydrology Branch of the Division of Waste Management of the Office of Nuclear Material Safety and Safeguards. In this position he is responsible for the development and application of performance assessment methodologies for low-level and high-level waste disposal sites as well as for materials sites undergoing decommissioning through burial of contaminated soils and slags on site. Dr. Austin holds a BS in Chemical Engineering from Purdue University, a Master's degree in Engineering Science from the University of California at Berkeley, and a PhD in Nuclear Engineering from North Carolina State University.

Samuel Goodhope is the Special Assistant Attorney General in the Office of the Attorney General, State of Texas. He is responsible for advising Attorney General Dan Morales on issues regarding federal facility (DOE and DOD) and federal program environmental cleanup, compliance, pollution prevention, and other policy issues. Mr. Goodhope served on Governor Ann Richards' Task Force on Economic Transition and has been involved with remediation issues at closing or realigned bases in Texas such as Bergstrom Air Force Base, Chase Naval Air Station, Dallas Naval Air Station, and Caswell Air Force Base. He holds an AB in Economics from the University of California at Berkeley and a JD from the Harvard Law School.

Joseph Nagel currently owns a small environmental consulting firm, Nagel Environmental Consulting. Prior to this he was Director of the Department of Environmental Quality for the State of Idaho. Mr. Nagel has also worked on environmental issues at the local and federal government level. He holds a BA in Philosophy and a Master's degree in History from Denver-St. Thomas, Denver, CO.

Donald Macdonald has served as the Executive Assistant to the Manager of the Idaho Operations Office since February of 1994. In this position he reports to and assists the Manager of the Idaho Operations Office in directing and overseeing the activities of the Idaho National Engineering Laboratory (INEL). Prior to this he was manager of the Buried Waste Program for the

DOE-ID where he was responsible for the management of a range of activities dedicated to remediating the environmental risks posed from the burial of radioactive and hazardous wastes at the INEL. Mr. Macdonald holds a Bachelor's degree in History and Political Science from Colorado College in Colorado Springs.

Louis Bogar is a consultant specializing in radiological site remediation and nuclear safety assessments. He is currently involved with the Waste Isolation Pilot Plant in assessing the operational readiness status. Mr. Bogar has a broad background in the management of nuclear safety and technology. He worked for the Westinghouse Electric Corporation for 28 years serving as Vice President at Westinghouse Materials Company of Ohio from 1986–1992. He retired from Westinghouse in September 1992. Mr. Bogar holds an SB in chemistry from the Massachusetts Institute of Technology where he also studied Nuclear Engineering at the graduate level.

Adam Babich is editor in-chief of ELR-The Environmental Law Reporter and directs the publications division of the Environmental Law Institute, a nonprofit, nonpartisan organization dedicated to improving environmental law through research, dialogue, and education. He is also an adjunct professor at the Georgetown University Law Center. While in private environmental law practice, Mr. Babich's clients included citizen's groups, municipalities, and members of the regulated community. He was the lead plaintiff's counsel on two citizen's suits about the Rocky Flats nuclear weapons plant. Mr. Babich holds a JD from the Yale Law School.

Elmer Akin is Chief of the Office of Health Assessment, Waste Management Division, Region IV, U.S. EPA. Prior to this he was Director of the Toxicology and Microbiology Division, Health Effects Research Laboratory, U.S. EPA, Cincinnati, OH.

Lokesh Chaturvedi is the Deputy Director of the Environmental Evaluation Group (EEG) of the New Mexico Institute of Mining and Technology, in Albuquerque, New Mexico. The EEG performs independent scientific evaluation of the Waste Isolation Pilot Plant (WIPP) on behalf of the State of New Mexico.

Tom Isaacs is the Executive Director of the Advisory Committee on External Regulation of Department of Energy Nuclear Safety.

David O'Very is the Attorney Advisor/Special Assistant to the Director, Office of Radiation and Indoor Air. Prior to this position he was a legal fellow with the Natural Resources Defense Council. He was the chief editor and contributing author for the book *Controlling the Atom in the Twenty-first Century* published in 1994.

Suzanne Rudzinski is the Director of the Office of Policy Analysis at the DOE Department of Environmental Management.

Milton Russell is the Director of the Joint Institute for Energy and Environment and Professor of Economics at the University of Tennessee. He was previously Assistant Administrator for Policy, Planning, and Evaluation at the U.S. EPA.

PRIORITY SETTING, TIMING AND STAGING OF ENVIRONMENTAL MANAGEMENT ACTIVITIES WORKSHOP

Carol J. Henry is currently the Science and Policy Director of the Office of Integrated Risk Management at the Department of Energy (DOE). She is responsible for the development of major policies, systems and guidelines for DOE's Environmental Management risk management programs and activities and she reports directly to the Assistant Secretary for Environmental Management. From 1992–94 Dr. Henry was the Director of the Office of Environmental Health Hazard Assessment, California Environmental Protection Agency. She was previously the Executive Director of the International Life Sciences Institute's Risk Science Institute in Washington, DC. Dr. Henry holds a PhD in Microbiology from the University of Pittsburgh and has done post doctoral work at the Max Planck Institute in Tubingen, at Princeton University and at the Sloan Kettering Institute.

Douglas L. Weaver is Independent Review Program Manager at Sandia National Laboratories. He has 24 years experience in the management and operation of complex manufacturing facilities and is currently applying this experience to support a DOE Environmental Management Program need for independent reviews (Red Teams) of programs and projects. Mr. Weaver has led Red Team reviews and evaluations at the Rocky Flats Plant, Oak Ridge National Laboratory Isotopes Facilities, Mound Plant, Los Alamos National Laboratory, Lawrence Livermore National Laboratory, Sandia National Laboratories and Brookhaven National Laboratory. He has participated in reviews of other plants including Hanford, Savannah River, and Pinellas. Mr. Weaver also provides planning and management consulting support to several elements within the Department of Energy. [He was a speaker at the previous workshop on Priority-Setting, Timing and Staging.]

Bob Anderson is Project Leader of the Prioritization, Environmental Health and Safety Division at Los Alamos National Laboratory.

Curtis C. Travis is Director of the Center for Risk Management at Oak Ridge National Laboratory. He is a Fellow of the International Society for Risk Analysis and a Senior Research Fellow with the Energy, Environment, and Resources Center at the University of Tennessee. His research interests include exposure assessment, pharmacokinetics, environmental policy, science-based risk analysis and effectiveness of environmental technologies. Dr. Travis serves on numerous advisory boards and holds a PhD in applied mathematics from the University of California at Davis.

John S. Applegate is the James B. Helmer Jr., Professor of Law at the

University of Cincinnati College of Law, where he teaches environmental law, administrative law, and torts. He chairs the Fernald Citizens Task Force, a site-specific advisory board established by the US Department of Energy to advise it on the central environmental issues arising out of the clean-up of the formal nuclear weapons facility in Fernald, Ohio. He is also a member of the DOE's Environmental Management Advisory Board. Professor Applegate previously practiced law with the firm of Covington & Burling in Washington, DC. He received his JD from Harvard Law School.

Susan Wiltshire is Vice President of JK Research Associates, a consulting firm specializing in public policy formulation, strategic planning and citizen involvement for technical programs. Ms. Wiltshire is Chairman of the US EPA Advisory Committee on the Waste Isolation Pilot Plant and a member of EPA's Advisory Committee on Radiation Site Cleanup Regulation. Her current appointments include membership on the Committee on Technical Bases for Yucca Mountain Standards and the Committee to Review New York State's Siting and Methodology Selection for Low-Level Radioactive Waste Disposal, which she chairs.

Toby Michelena is Coordinator of Tank Waste Remediation Systems at the Washington State Department of Ecology.

Lee W. Merkhofer is currently a Principal at Applied Decision Analysis, Inc. and has more than 20 years of experience in the research, teaching, and application of formal decision and risk analysis. Best known for his analyses of public health and environmental issues, he also serves commercial clients in risk analysis and planning. Dr. Merkhofer's research includes analyses of national air quality standards, energy and waste facility siting decisions, and space mission planning. Before joining ADA he was Associate Director and Manager of Research Programs, Decision Analysis Group, SRI International. He holds a PhD in engineering-economic systems from Stanford University.

Brian Costner is Director of the Energy Research Foundation. He regularly works to interpret the Savannah River Site environmental , safety, health, and production activities within the context of overall Department of Energy programs and policies. Mr. Costner was a member of the working group which established the charter for the Savannah River Site Citizens Advisory Board and is now a member of that Board. He also helps design and implement many activities with the Military Production Network, and is a member of the Medical University of South Carolina's Environmental Risk Management Advisory Committee. He is also a member of the South Carolina

Research Authority's Reclamation and Reduction of Nuclear Residuals Advisory Board.

Julie D'Ambrosia is a Program Director of EnviroTech Associates, a consulting firm providing technical support to the Department of Energy's Office of Environmental Restoration, where she facilitates technical and programmatic information exchange between the Office of Environmental Restoration, external organizations, and the public. She has nearly 20 years of technical experience in DOE's waste management and environmental restoration programs. From 1991–94, Ms. D'Ambrosia served as a technical assistant to the Deputy Assistant Secretary for Environmental Restoration. Prior to that, she was responsible for management of high level waste and transuranic waste at DOE's Savannah River Site, worked at DOE headquarters as the Waste Operations program manager for the Hanford, Idaho, Albuquerque, and Nevada sites, and performed research on plutonium chemistry at the Hanford site.

Robert N. Ferguson is Oversight Administrator at the Idaho National Engineering Laboratory and is directly responsible to the Governor of the State of Idaho. He is a senior level nuclear professional with over 30 years of diverse, in-depth experience in the nuclear industry. His expertise includes reactor operations, design engineering, project engineering, project management, and corporate management. His extensive experience demonstrates strong capabilities in project management and assessments. Mr. Ferguson was previously Senior Engineer at Science Applications International Corporation; Vice President of LRS Consultants Incorporated; and Vice President of Engineering & Systems at Energy Incorporated. He holds a BS in mechanical engineering from the University of Wyoming and an MBA from the University of Idaho.

Mark Gilbertson is Program Director of the Office of Integrated Risk Management at the US Department of Energy.

WORKSHOP ON UTILIZATION OF SCIENCE, ENGINEERING, AND TECHNOLOGY

Carol J. Henry is the Science and Policy Director of the Office of Integrated Risk Management at the Department of Energy (DOE). She is responsible for the development of major policies, systems and guidelines for DOE's Environmental Management risk management programs and activities and she reports directly to the Assistant Secretary for Environmental Management. From 1992–94 Dr. Henry was the Director of the Office of Environmental Health Hazard Assessment, California Environmental Protection Agency. She was previously the Executive Director of the International Life Sciences Institute's Risk Science Institute in Washington, DC. Dr. Henry holds a PhD in Microbiology from the University of Pittsburgh and has done post doctoral work at the Max Planck Institute in Tubingen, at Princeton University and at the Sloan Kettering Institute.

John (Mac) Lankford is a staff member at the Department of Energy.

Teresa Fryberger is a staff member at the Department of Energy.

Harry D. Harmon is presently technical director of the High Level Management Division of the Westinghouse Savannah River Company where he oversees all divisional research and development efforts for the company and for the Department of Energy. Dr. Harmon has held research and managerial positions in many divisions of the Savannah River Laboratory since he joined the project in 1973. Prior to the Savannah River Company, Dr. Harmon was assistant professor of Chemistry at Walters State Community College in Morristown, TN. He holds a BS in Chemistry from Carson-Newman College in Jefferson City, TN, and a PhD in Inorganic and Nuclear Chemistry from the University of Tennessee in 1971.

Walter Kovalick is the Director of the Technology Innovation Office, Office of Solid Waste and Emergency Response, United States Environmental Protection Agency. Prior to this position he served as Acting Deputy Administrator for the Office of Solid Waste and Emergency Response. For five years, until December 1989, he was the Deputy Director of the Superfund program. He joined EPA in 1970 from one of its predecessor agencies. Dr. Kovalick is a member of the American Society for Public Administration, the Institute for Industrial Engineers, and the Academy of Management. He holds a MBA from Harvard Business School and a PhD in Public Administration and Policy from Virginia Polytechnic Institute.

John B. Carberry is currently director of Environmental Technology for E.I. DuPont in Wilmington, DE. He has held a series of management and developmental positions within DuPont since joining them in 1965, and Mr. Carberry presently represents DuPont as the U.S. Regional Coordinating Partner in the IMS Initiative for Cleaner Technologies. In addition, he has also served on numerous advisory boards and committees for universities and organizations. Mr. Carberry holds a BS and an MS in Chemical Engineering from Cornell University and an MBA from the University of Delaware in 1974. He is a member of the National Academy of Sciences.

Rebecca Tyrrell Parkin is concurrently the Director of Scientific, Professional and Section Affairs at the American Public Health Association and the President of Beccam Services where she specializes in occupational and environmental health, and policy analysis. She has also been an Adjunct Assistant Professor in the Department of Environmental and Community Medicine, University of Medicine and Dentistry of New Jersey, since 1984. Dr. Parkin was previously Assistant Commissioner in the Division of Occupational and Environmental Health, New Jersey Department of Health; Epidemiologist, Division of Birth Defects and Developmental Disabilities, Center for Environmental Health and Injury Control at the Centers for Disease Control; and Chief of the Environmental Health Program, New Jersey Department of Health. She holds and MPH in Environmental Health and a PhD in Epidemiology from Yale University.

J. Robert (Bob) Hightower is director of the Center for Waste Management and manager of the Integrated Mixed Waste Program of the Energy Systems Waste Management Organization in Oak Ridge, Tennessee. His responsibilities involve management of all mixed waste activities and coordination of all technology development activities for all waste types sponsored by the Office of Waste Management on the Oak Ridge Reservation. Dr. Hightower holds a BS from the University of Mississippi and a PhD from Tulane University, both in Chemical Engineering.

Gretchen H. McCabe is currently senior research scientist with the Battelle Company in Seattle, WA, where she specializes in assessing environmental issues from technical and public policy perspectives. Her recent work includes analyzing public, regulatory, and technology user acceptance of deploying new waste management and environmental remediation technologies. Prior to Battelle, Ms. McCabe spent five years at the Congressional Office of Technology Assessment (OTA) working in the environmental technology and policy arena. Ms. McCabe holds a BA in geology and an MS in political science from the Massachusetts Institute of Technology.

Roger P. (Pat) Whitfield is retired from the Department of Energy as the deputy assistant secretary for environmental restoration. He holds a BS and an ME from the University of Alabama and an MBA from Florida State University.

Christopher J. Nagel is a co-founder and Executive Vice President of Science and Technology of Molten Metal Technology, Inc., a company engaged in the development and commercialization of an innovative chemical processing technology, known as Catalytic Extraction Processing (CEP). From 1986 to 1991, Dr. Nagel was a doctoral student in the School of Chemical Engineering at M.I.T. Dr. Nagel was employed by USX (previously U.S. Steel) where he served as Manager of Energy Conservation and Coordination from 1982 to 1986. Dr. Nagel holds a ScD in Chemical Engineering from M.I.T. and a BS in Chemical Engineering from Michigan Technological University.

David Rubenson is a senior public policy analyst at RAND in Santa Monica, California. At RAND since 1980, Mr. Rubenson has worked on research projects involving energy, environmental, and natural resource policy. Recently he has focused his efforts on the environmental program of the Department of Defense and on U.S. environmental policy including an analysis of 1990 Clean Air Act's requirements for Automobile Inspection and Maintenance (I&M). Mr. Rubenson holds an MS in Physics from the University of Pennsylvania and an MBA from the University of California, Los Angeles.

Edwin H. Clark II is President of Clean Sites, Inc., in Alexandria, VA. He is former Secretary of the Delaware Department of Natural Resources and Environmental Control, Vice President of the Conservation Foundation, and Acting Assistant Administrator of the pesticides and toxic substances program in the Environmental Protection Agency. He holds a PhD in applied economics from Princeton University.

INTEGRATION OF SCIENCE, ENGINEERING AND HEALTH IN PROGRAM IMPLEMENTATION

Daniel A. Abramowicz is Manager of the Environmental Laboratory at General Electric Corporate Research and Development. He is responsible for developing GE's environmental research program, including remediation, pollution prevention waste minimization, and product stewardship efforts. He is concurrently an Adjunct Professor in the Department of Biology at Rensselaer Polytechnic Institute. Dr. Abramowicz joined GE Corporate R&D in 1984 as Staff Chemist; in 1988 he became Manager of the Environmental Technology Program, and in 1992 Manager of Bioremediation Branch, before succeeding to his current position in 1993. He serves on the Advisory Board of the Idaho National Engineering Laboratory and on the Executive Board of the New York State Hazardous Waste Management. Dr. Abramowicz has published extensively and holds an MS and a PhD in physical chemistry from Princeton University.

John S. Applegate is the James B. Helmer Jr., Professor of Law at the University of Cincinnati College of Law, where he teaches environmental law, administrative law, and torts. He chairs the Fernald Citizens Task Force, a site-specific advisory board established by the US Department of Energy to provide advise on the central environmental issues arising from the clean-up of the formal nuclear weapons facility in Fernald, Ohio. He is also a member of the DOE's Environmental Management Advisory Board. Professor Applegate previously practiced law with the firm of Covington & Burling in Washington, DC. He received his JD from Harvard Law School. [He was a speaker at the previous workshop on Priority-Setting, Timing and Staging.]

Deborah R. Bennett is Staff Member of the Environmental Management/Red Team of the US Department of Energy at Los Alamos National Laboratory (LANL) since 1992. She has seventeen years experience with commercial, defense, and space nuclear power systems, and assessments of Department of Energy facilities and processes. Ms. Bennett has worked at LANL since 1978 when she joined the Gas-Cooled Fast Breeder Reactor Experimental Program. Subsequent positions included work in Carbide Fuel Development; Technical Assistance to Nuclear Regulatory Commission; Technical Assistance to Office of Defense Energy Projects, DOE Office of Nuclear Energy; SP-100 Nuclear Subsystems, Manager and Section Leader; and New Production Reactor Safety Project Office. She holds a BS and is pursuing an MS in mechanical engineering from the University of New Mexico.

Ken Glozer is Senior Advisor to the Assistant Secretary for Environmental Management-Thomas P. Grumbly. Mr. Glozer is responsible for the design and implementation of initiatives to make the cleanup program efficient and effective. His prior position was Deputy Associate Director, Office of Management and Budget in the natural resource environment and energy area. Mr. Glozer has been a senior ranked federal career official for 20 years and has extensive experience with reforming and restructuring across a large number of federal programs and agencies. Prior to his federal career, he was with Peat, Marwick, Mitchell & Company. He holds an MBA from George Washington University.

Rear Admiral Richard J. Guimond is the Principal Deputy Assistant Secretary for Environmental Management at the US Department of Energy. A Commissioned Officer in the US Public Health Service since 1970, he was appointed Assistant Surgeon General to C. Everett Koop in 1989. Prior to assuming his duties at the DOE, Rear Admiral (RADM) Guimond served on extended detail to the Environmental Protection Agency (EPA) for most of his career. He joined EPA at its inception and served in a number of different capacities, the most notable being the Acting Assistant Administrator for Solid Waste and Emergency Response and the Deputy Assistant Administrator for Solid Waste and Emergency Response. RADM Guimond is the recipient of numerous awards and honors, and holds an Master of Engineering from Rensselaer Polytechnic Institute in 1970 and an MS in environmental health from Harvard University in 1973.

Kevin Holtzclaw is Senior Program Manager of General Electric Company's Environmental Remediation Program since July 1991. Prior to this position, he was Manager of GE Corporate Environmental Programs in the Mid-Atlantic and Southeast Regional Office. Mr. Holtzclaw joined GE Nuclear Energy Division in 1969 working in the area of Nuclear Fuel Research and Development. In the succeeding 18 years with GE Nuclear he had a variety of assignments in the areas of design, safety and environmental analyses, licensing and risk assessment. Mr. Holtzclaw was heavily involved in the evaluations of the Three Mile Island and Chernobyl Accidents. In late 1987, he transferred to GE's corporate office to manage hazardous waste remediation programs where he was responsible for a number of Superfund site cleanups. He holds an MS in mechanical engineering from the University of California at Berkeley.

Richard C. Marty is Senior Engineer Specialist in Risk Assessment and Waste Management at Jason Associates Corporation. His current work involves supporting Rocky Flats in consolidating Operable Units and developing a site-wide treatment strategy for contaminated groundwater. He has extensive experience in the design of cleanup strategies for sites contaminated with hazardous and radioactive constituents. His Independent Technical Review

Team experience has included reviews of projects at Brookhaven National Laboratory and Los Alamos National Laboratory. Dr. Marty was also the leader of special projects and shoreline assessment teams assessing damage and designing cleanup strategies for Exxon Operations following the *Exxon Valdez* incident. He has supported environmental characterization and cleanup design efforts for a wide variety of DOE and private sector clients. He holds an BS in biology and an MS in geology from Portland State University and a PhD in geology and geochemistry from Rice University.

Henry E. (Hank) McGuire is Vice President of Business Development with Scientific Ecology Group, a subsidiary of Westinghouse Corporation. He is responsible for western region business development both inside and outside of the Department of Energy complex. Mr. McGuire has over 25 years experience in the treatment storage and disposal of municipal, hazardous and radioactive mixed waste, most recently as Vice President for Waste Management activities for the Westinghouse Hanford Company. He holds a BS in civil engineering from Worcester Polytechnic Institute and an MS in environmental engineering from Loyola Marymount University, with additional graduate work in chemical engineering and industrial waste treatment at Vanderbilt University.

Philip A. Palmer is Senior Environmental Fellow at I.E. du Pont de Nemours & Company in the DuPont Chemicals Core Resources Section of the Corporate Remediation Group. He has over 15 years of experience in the field of hazardous waste management, the last 5 of which has been devoted to remediation technology development. He currently heads a group of 40 people that is evaluating remediation technologies and he oversees development and pilot testing of new technologies on DuPont sites and assessment of the company's remediation technology needs. He served as a chairman and member of the Chemical Manufacturers Association RCRA Regulations Task Force from the inception of RCRA until 1990. Mr. Palmer holds an MS in chemical engineering from Cornell University and an MS in environmental engineering from Drexel University. [He is a member of the Subcommittee on Utilization of Science, Engineering and Technology.]

Gail M. Pesyna is the Deputy Assistant Secretary for Management and Finance in the Office of Environmental Management. She is responsible for financial management, information systems, procurement, and personnel and administrative management activities for the Environmental Management program. Previously, Dr. Pesyna was Business Operations Manager for DuPont Printing and Publishing. She has a background in operations management, sales management, marketing, and new business development in DuPont's "high-tech" businesses, including Pharmaceuticals and Medical Diagnostics.

Prior to 1981, Dr. Pesyna worked as a science and technology policy analyst for the US Congress and a budget examiner for the US Office of Management and Budget. She holds a PhD in analytical chemistry and computer science from Cornell University, and is a member of Sigma Xi and Phi Beta Kappa.

Patricia A. Rivers is the Assistant Deputy Under Secretary of Defense for Environmental Cleanup in the Office of the Secretary of Defense, US Department of Defense. She is responsible for developing environmental cleanup policy for Defense activities worldwide and for overseeing implementation of that policy by the Military Departments. Prior to this position, she was Chief of the Environmental Division in the Office of the Inspector General, US Department of Defense, from 1990 to January 1994. Ms. Rivers served for thirteen years, beginning in 1977, with the Department of Navy in positions as facilities engineer, environmental engineer, and program manager for the Navy's environmental cleanup program. Ms. Rivers's last assignment in the Department of Navy was in the office of the Chief of Naval Operations, Installation Restoration Branch, where she developed policy for the environmental cleanup program. She holds a BS in civil engineering and is a registered professional engineer in the Commonwealth of Virginia.

Philip Thullen is Program Manager for Independent Technical Reviews (ITR) at Los Alamos National Laboratory, Environmental Management Programs. Dr. Thullen established Independent Review or "Red Teams" as a Los Alamos program in June, 1991, and since then, he has led or participated in over 20 ITRs and numerous related spin-off activities. Reviews are typically focused on environmental restoration, waste management, and facility transition. Before joining Los Alamos in 1976, Dr. Thullen was Assistant and Associate Professor of Mechanical Engineering in the Thermal and Fluid Sciences Division of the Mechanical Engineering Department at MIT. Dr. Thullen holds an SM in mechanical engineering and a ScD from MIT. [He was a participant in the previous workshop on Priority Setting, Timing and Staging.]

Douglas L. Weaver is Independent Review Program Manager at Sandia National Laboratories. He has 24 years experience in the management and operation of complex manufacturing facilities and is currently applying this experience to support a DOE Environmental Management Program need for independent reviews (Red Teams) of programs and projects. Mr. Weaver has led Red Team reviews and evaluations at the Rocky Flats Plant, Oak Ridge National Laboratory Isotopes Facilities, Mound Plant, Los Alamos National Laboratory, Lawrence Livermore National Laboratory, Sandia National Laboratories and Brookhaven National Laboratory. He has participated in reviews of other plants including Hanford, Savannah River, and Pinellas. Mr. Weaver also provides planning and management consulting support to several elements within the Department of Energy. [He was a speaker at the previous workshop on Priority-Setting, Timing and Staging.]